MW01626243

THE *Magna Book* OF

~

VAN GOGH

~

A BEAUTIFUL GUIDE TO SOME OF VAN GOGH'S FINEST WORKS

DEDICATION

For Susan and Adam

Editor: Fleur Robertson
Editorial Assistance: Kirsty Wheeler
Original Design Concept: Peter Bridgewater
Design: Stonecastle Graphics Ltd
Director of Production: Gerald Hughes
Production: Ruth Arthur, Sally Connolly, Neil Randles
Typesetter: Julie Smith

Jacket: *Irises* (detail)
Private collection

CLB 3142
This 1994 edition published by Magna Books,
Magna Road, Wigston, Leicester LE18 4ZH

Printed and bound in Singapore.

ISBN 1 85422 544 8

THE *Magna Book* OF VAN GOGH

JULIET RODWAY

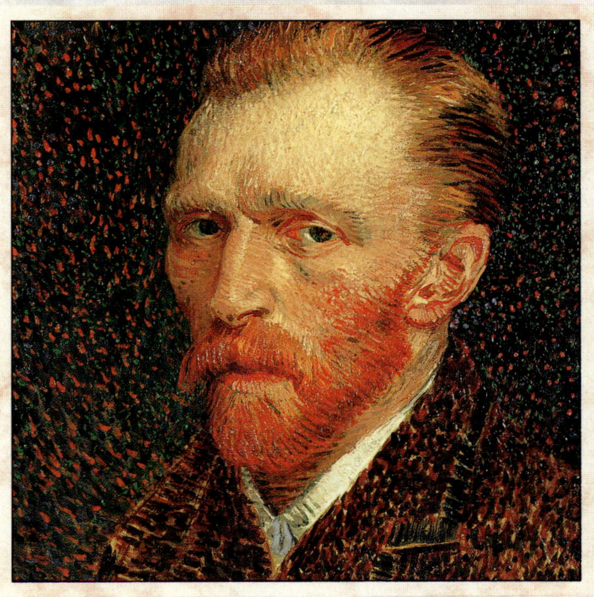

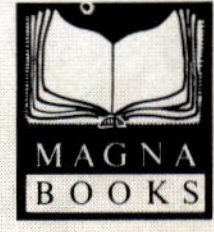

Introduction

The story of Vincent van Gogh's short but remarkable career is one of the most fascinating in the history of art. In just ten years he progressed from primitive draughtsman to supreme colourist, producing over two thousand paintings, drawings and prints. Many of the most famous – like *Sunflowers*, *Vincent's Chair* and *Irises* – were painted in the last two-and-a-half years of his life. Today his pictures fetch record prices at auction, but during his lifetime Vincent succeeded in selling only one painting. Sometimes he even had difficulty giving his work away – one gift was used to block up a hole in a chicken coop!

Vincent van Gogh was born on 30 March, 1853, at Groot-Zundert in Holland, the son of a Reformed Church pastor. He was an introverted boy, with a deep love of nature, but he had no outstanding artistic ability. At sixteen he was employed by his uncle's art gallery, Goupil and Co., and stationed in The Hague, London and Paris. In 1873, whilst working in the London branch, he fell in love with his landlady's daughter, Eugenie Loyer. When she rejected him, Vincent over-reacted and became extremely morose, revealing the first signs of the mental instability that would plague him for the rest of his life. His inability to overcome his emotions cost him his job, and after short spells as a teacher and bookshop assistant, he decided to enter the Church. He passionately wanted to become a preacher, but after failing to obtain the necessary qualifications, he had to settle for a temporary appointment as a missionary in the Borinage, the Belgian coal-mining district. Vincent threw himself into his work with alarming zeal, giving away his clothes, food and money to help the poor. Unfortunately, this extreme behaviour was viewed as unsuitable and he again lost his job.

It was at this time that he began drawing, initially making tentative studies of miners. Through this, at twenty-seven, Vincent found his true vocation. He applied himself relentlessly, with the aim of becoming a painter of peasants like the French artist, Jean-Francois Millet. It was a formidable task, but with the financial and professional help of his brother Theo, an art dealer, he hoped to succeed. Of even greater value, though, was the emotional support Theo gave him over the years, sustained by almost daily correspondence.

From 1880-86 Vincent concentrated on improving his skills, tutored briefly by his cousin, the artist Anton Mauve. However, his difficult temperament meant that he soon fell out with people and much of his development was due to his own wide-ranging study of art and literature. The biggest outside influence on his work was the Impressionist movement, which he discovered in 1886, and which resulted in him lightening his colours and abandoning the moralising tone of his Dutch period. He still wanted to paint pictures that 'touched' people, but now by using heightened colour to express 'feeling'. His most successful works in this style were painted at Arles, where he went in 1888. Here, inspired by the magical southern light, he painted canvas after canvas in vivid colours and on all subjects – from orchards in bloom to street corners, from starry skies to little children.

Vincent had dreamt of establishing an artists' colony in Arles – working in harmony with nature in imitation of the Japanese artists he so admired – but the punishing schedule he had set himself soon took its toll. After the painter Gauguin's disasterous visit, his work was increasingly interrupted by bouts of mental illness, forcing him to an asylum. On 27 July, 1890, his seemingly indomitable spirit, which had taken him so far in such a brief time, broke: he committed suicide.

Vincent suffered much during his career, yet the overwhelming feeling in his paintings is one of exuberance, of sheer delight in life's riches. Perhaps, in the end, that was his greatest triumph.

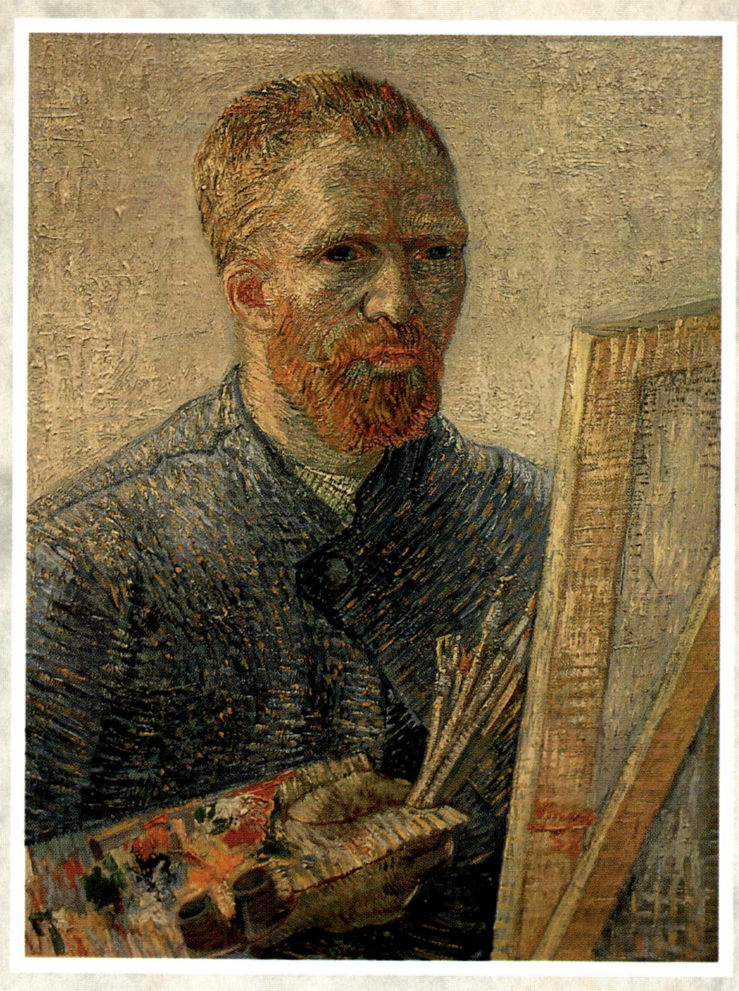

Self-Portait as a Painter

The inclusion of his easel and palette in this 1888 self-portrait suggests that Van Gogh felt he had at last become a true painter. His best work was yet to come, but his decision eight years earlier to abandon his religious studies in favour of art was finally being justified.

Remarkably for someone with no recognised talent, Vincent was determined from the first to be a major painter. He passionately devoted his life to this cause, often with little regard for his own health or well-being.

In this work, as in most of his paintings, Vincent was seeking a deeper truth than mere visual exactness. With some foreboding, he described the portrait as 'the face of Death'. He died just over two years later, but not before he had produced a magnificent body of work.

1888
66 x 51 cm
Oil on canvas
Vincent van Gogh Museum, Amsterdam

The Potato Eaters

Vincent was nearly halfway through his artistic career when he completed this, his largest and most complex figure painting. Only after five years studying peasants at work did he feel capable of producing a full-scale composition worthy of comparison with his hero, the French artist Millet. As in his preaching, Vincent wanted to console the poor. By painting the De Groot family eating their meagre supper, he aimed to give 'dignity to manual labour'. He specifically used dark, earthy colours and a crude painting style to reflect the peasants' primitive situation.

Vincent thought highly of this work all his life, but Theo could find no buyer for it in Paris, where the lighter colours of the Impressionists made Vincent's work seem abysmally gloomy.

1885
82 x 114 cm
Oil on canvas
Vincent van Gogh Museum, Amsterdam

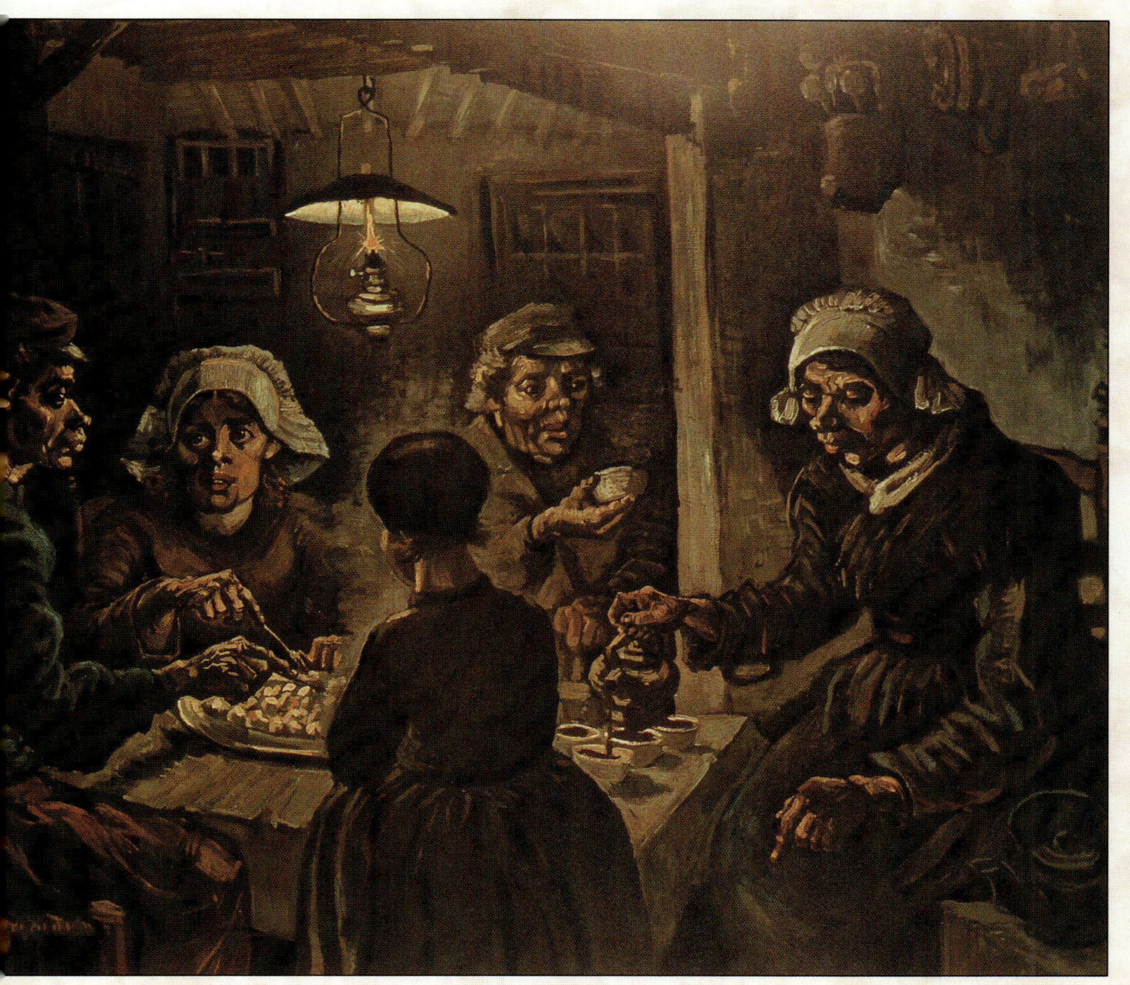

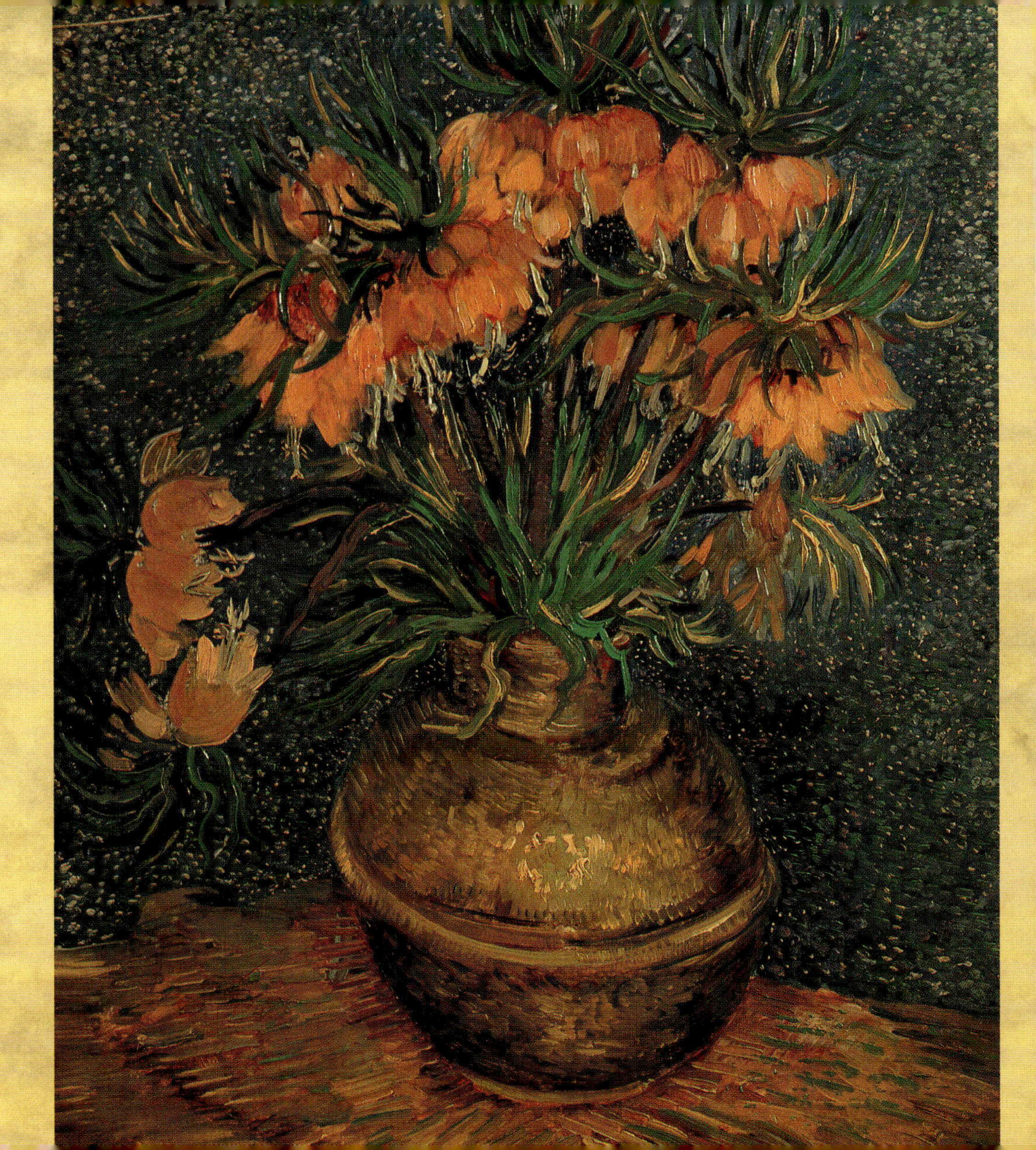

Still Life with Fritillaries

In March 1886, following several months' study at the Antwerp Academy of Fine Art, Vincent joined his brother Theo in Paris, then the centre of the modern art world. Space was severely limited in Theo's tiny flat on the Rue Laval, so Vincent initially concentrated on painting still lifes, producing over thirty flower pictures in 1886 alone.

Mixing with Europe's most progressive artists and seeing Impressionism at first-hand transformed Vincent's work. The dark hues of his Dutch style were banished forever and replaced with lighter, more exotic tints. He experimented feverishly, filling his canvases with a greater variety of brushstrokes and vibrant colour contrasts, as in this dazzling study of golden fritillaries against a speckled blue background.

1887
74 x 61 cm
Oil on canvas
Musee d'Orsay, Paris

The Park at Asnières

Whilst living in Paris, Vincent avoided the inner-city areas, preferring to paint in the more open suburbs. Asnières was a favourite haunt, and he often painted there with his colleagues, Paul Signac and Emile Bernard.

Keen to absorb the latest artistic trends, Vincent painted this landscape of lovers in a park using only tiny flecks of paint – a style he derived from Signac and Georges Seurat. When viewed from a certain distance, the dots blend in the spectator's eye to create the painting's particular forms and colours. He found this technique excellent for depicting the effects of light, particularly dappled sunlight. It was in Asnières' leafy quarters that Vincent's desire to express everything he painted in terms of pure colour first took tangible shape.

1887
76 x 113 cm
Oil on canvas
Vincent van Gogh Museum, Amsterdam

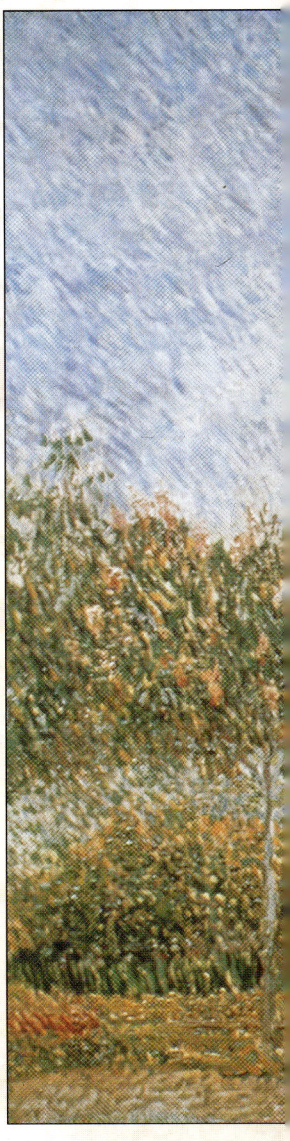

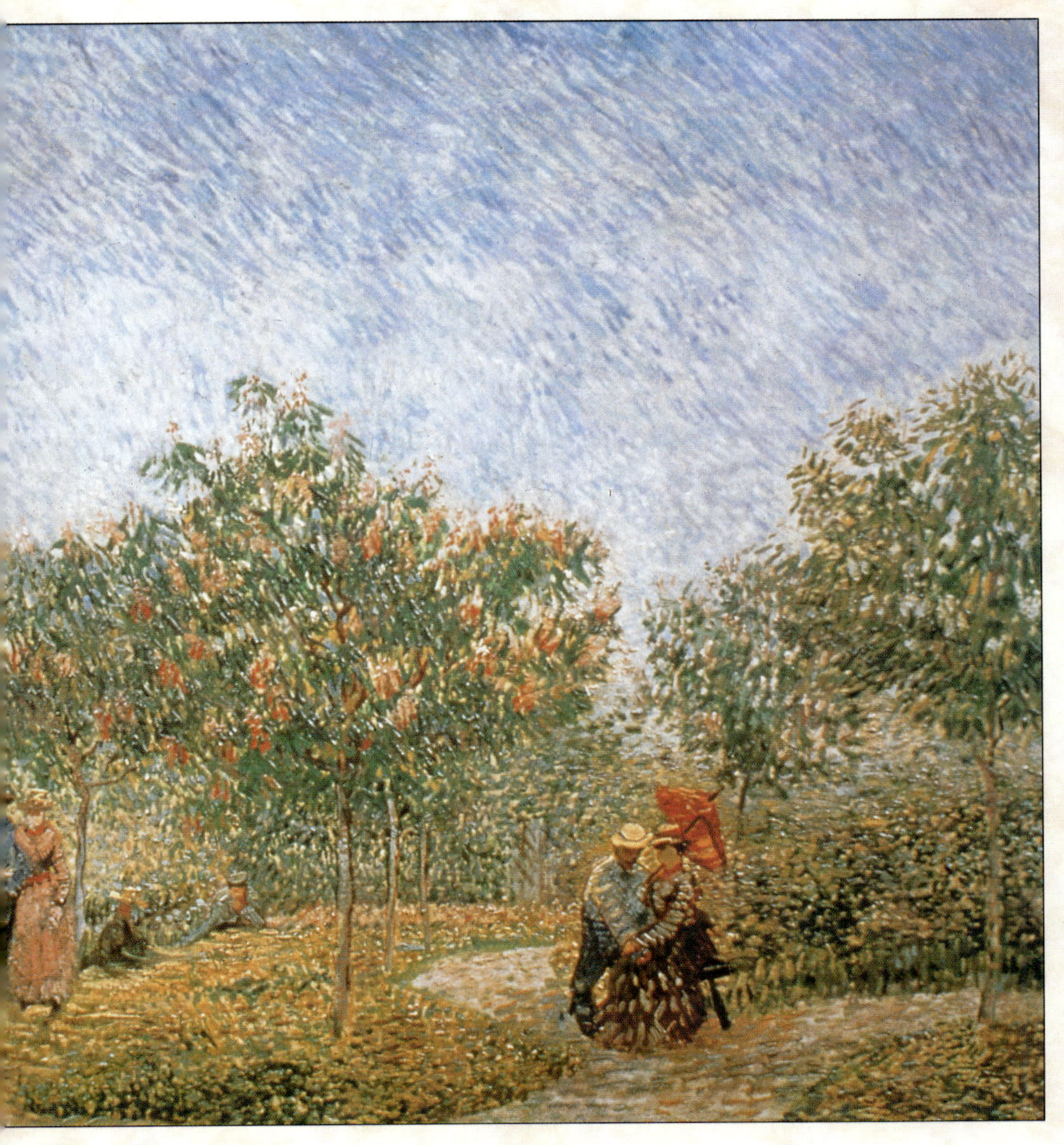

Portrait of Pére Tanguy

Vincent painted this intricate portrait in exchange for art materials. Julien Tanguy owned a small shop in Montmartre and often helped struggling artists in this manner. The shop was a popular meeting place: here Vincent met the painters Bernard, Signac and Cézanne, among others.

Vincent, grateful to Tanguy for his kindness, took great care with the painting, portraying him in a Buddha-like pose against a backdrop of Japanese prints. This was perhaps the highest compliment he could pay Tanguy, for Japan had come to represent Vincent's ideal world. He avidly collected Japanese prints, fascinated, as the Impressionists had been, by their strong, flat colours and unusual treatment of perspective. Tanguy was supposedly so taken with the portrait that he priced it too high to sell so as to keep it.

1887-88
92 x 75 cm
Oil on canvas
Musée Rodin, Paris

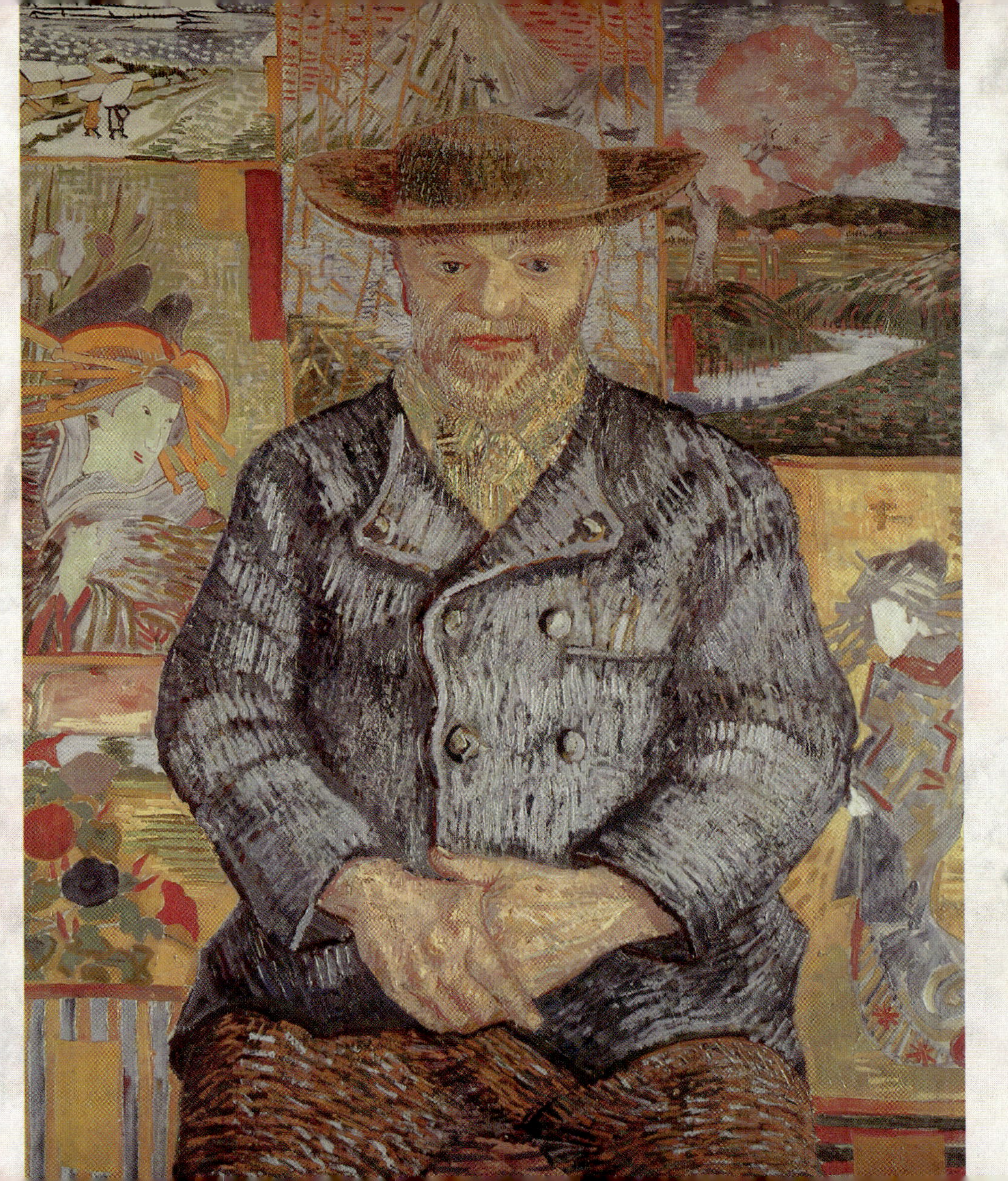

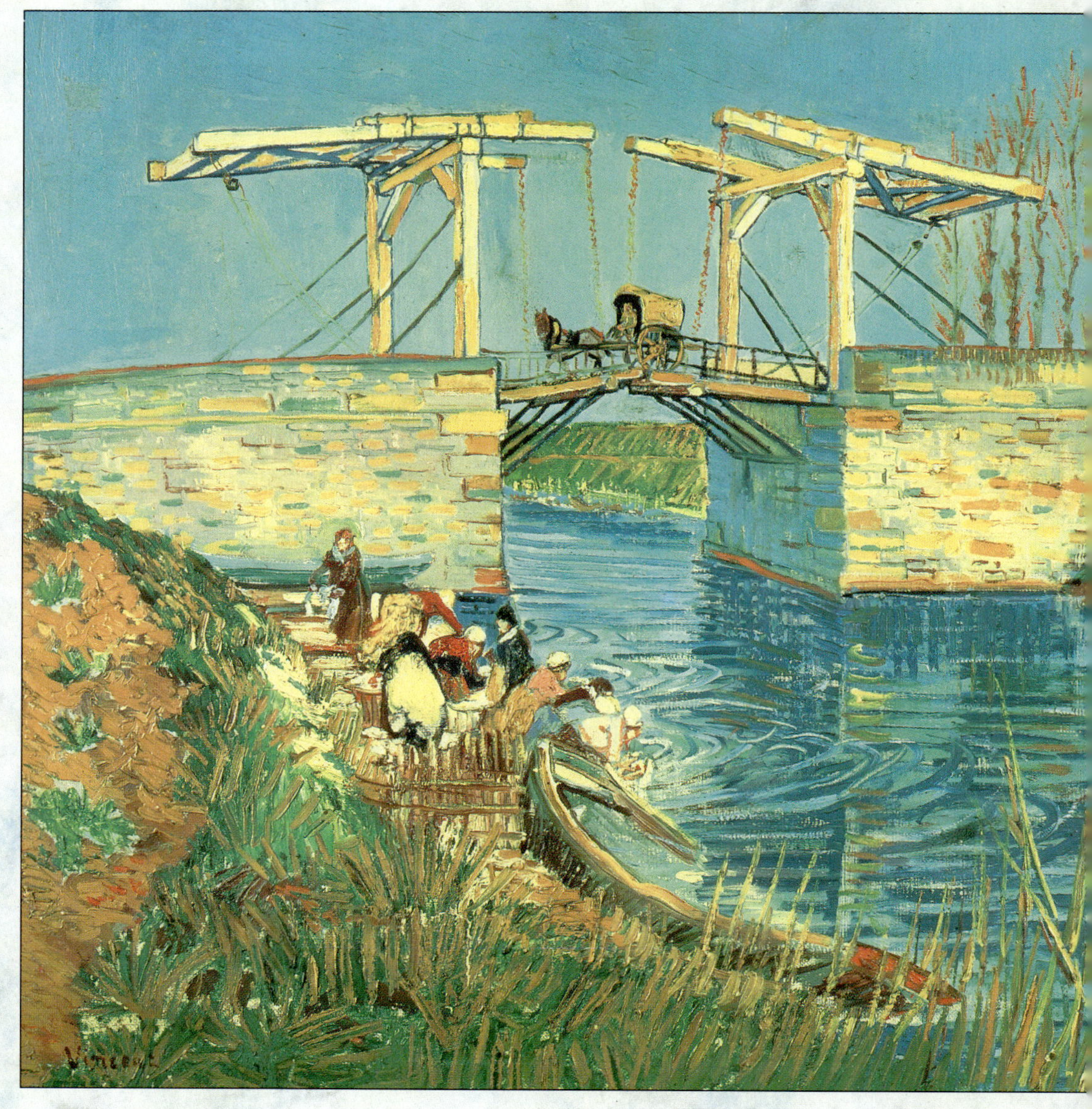
Vincent

Drawbridge with Carriage

In February 1888, Vincent left Paris for Arles in the south of France, 'the land of blue tones and gay colours', where he hoped to restore his health and create his own vision of Japan. In the luminous light Vincent saw colour even more intensely than before and it inspired him to work at a furious rate. In the spring he completed a series of canvases of orchards and painted several versions of this wooden drawbridge that spanned the Arles-to-Bouc canal – its Dutch-like structure may have reminded him of home. He purposely used strong, simple outlines and bright colours in the style of a Japanese woodcut. Pleased with his progress, Vincent wrote happily to Theo, 'I am convinced that I shall set my individuality free simply by staying on here'.

1888
54 x 65 cm
Oil on canvas
Kroller-Muller Museum, Otterlo

The Sower

Vincent spent his first summer in Arles exploring the Crau, an area of reclaimed marshland to the east of the town. Here, the harvesting of the wheatfields provided the subject for his second series of paintings. He worked happily in the fierce Midi sunshine, producing ten canvases in just one week. As always, it was the colours that captivated him. In *The Sower*, painted from his imagination, the sun's energising golden rays flood the canvas. Vincent intended this unlikely combination of harvest-time and seed-sowing to be more than just a simple landscape, he also wanted it to represent life's eternal cycle. In his view the figure scattering seed, based on Millet's famous *Sower*, was to symbolise renewal and the ripened wheat the promise of fulfillment.

1888
64 x 81 cm
Oil on canvas
Kroller-Muller Museum, Otterlo

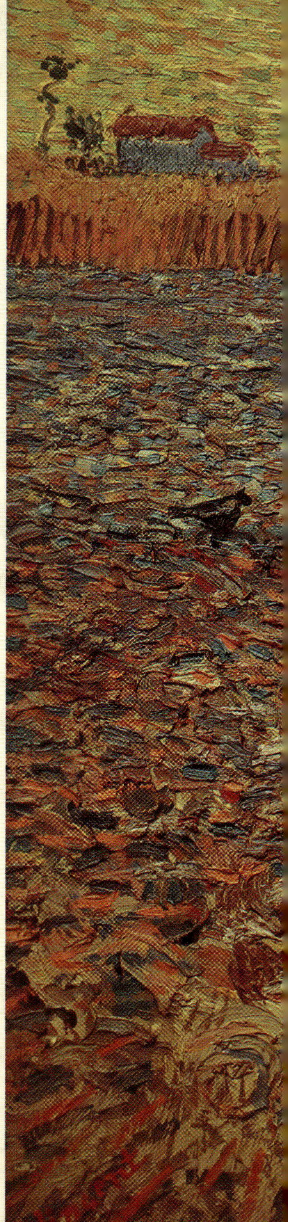

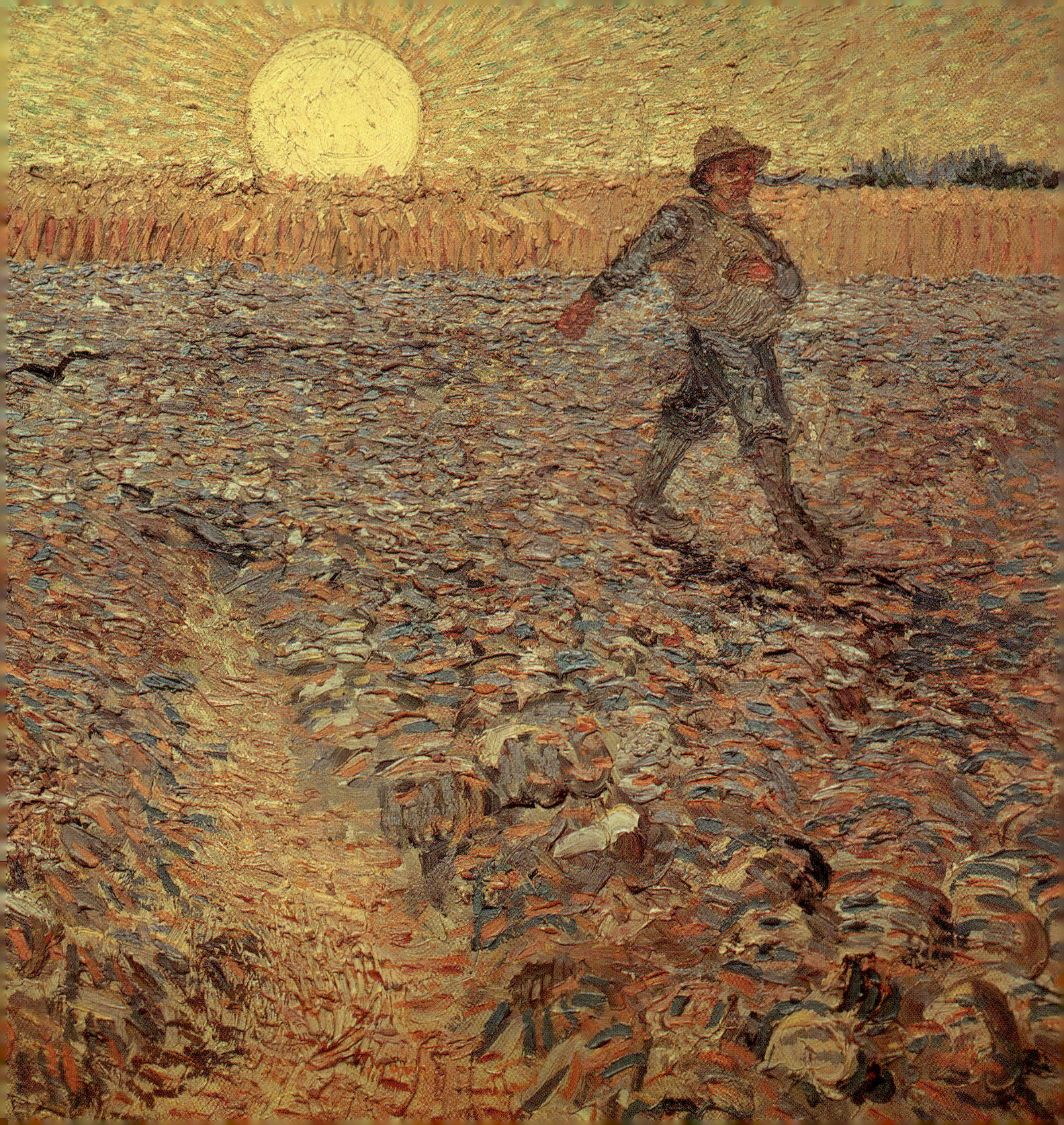

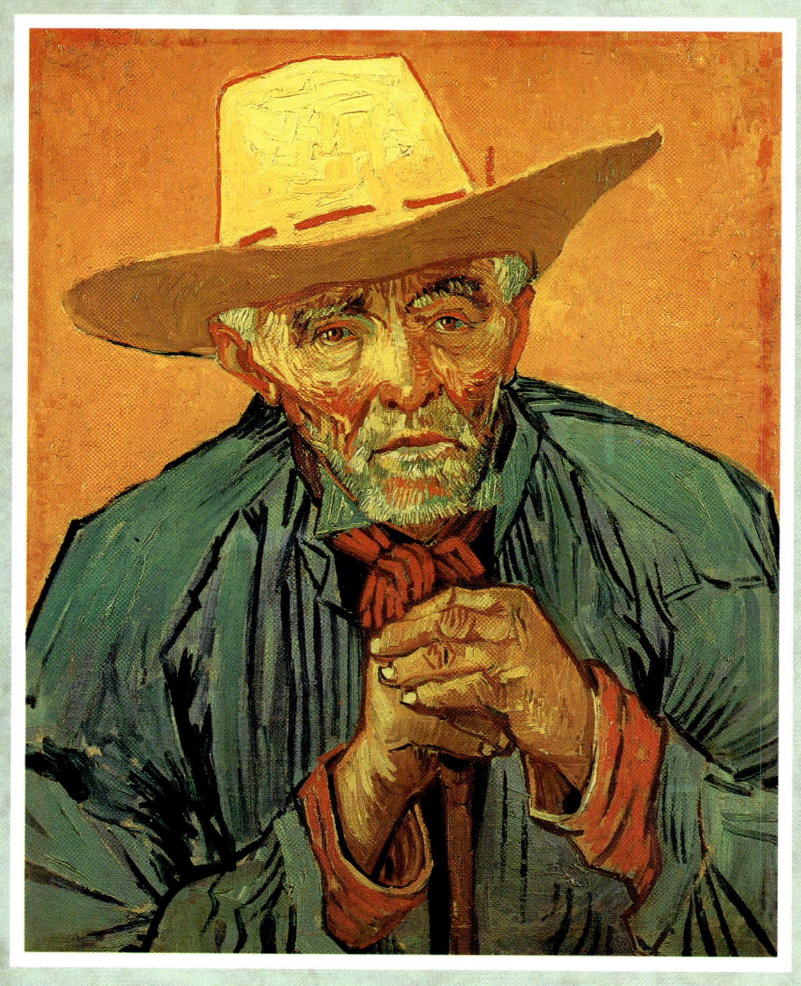

Portrait of Patience Escalier

Vincent attached great importance to portraiture. He preferred to paint ordinary working people, but as a newcomer to Arles he was short of models. Eager to remedy this – despite his meagre resources – he was prepared to offer his sitters payment. One grateful for the money was Patience Escalier, a local gardener and former Camargue cowhand. Vincent painted the old peasant twice, at the beginning and end of August, 1888. In this striking second version, Vincent delighted in depicting Escalier's weatherbeaten face, placing him against a vivid orange sky, as if bathed in the 'radiance of the setting sun'. The artist envisaged the canvas in Paris hanging beside polished society portraits – a contrast which would serve to highlight the radical earthiness of his own work all the more.

1888
69 x 56 cm
Oil on canvas
Private collection

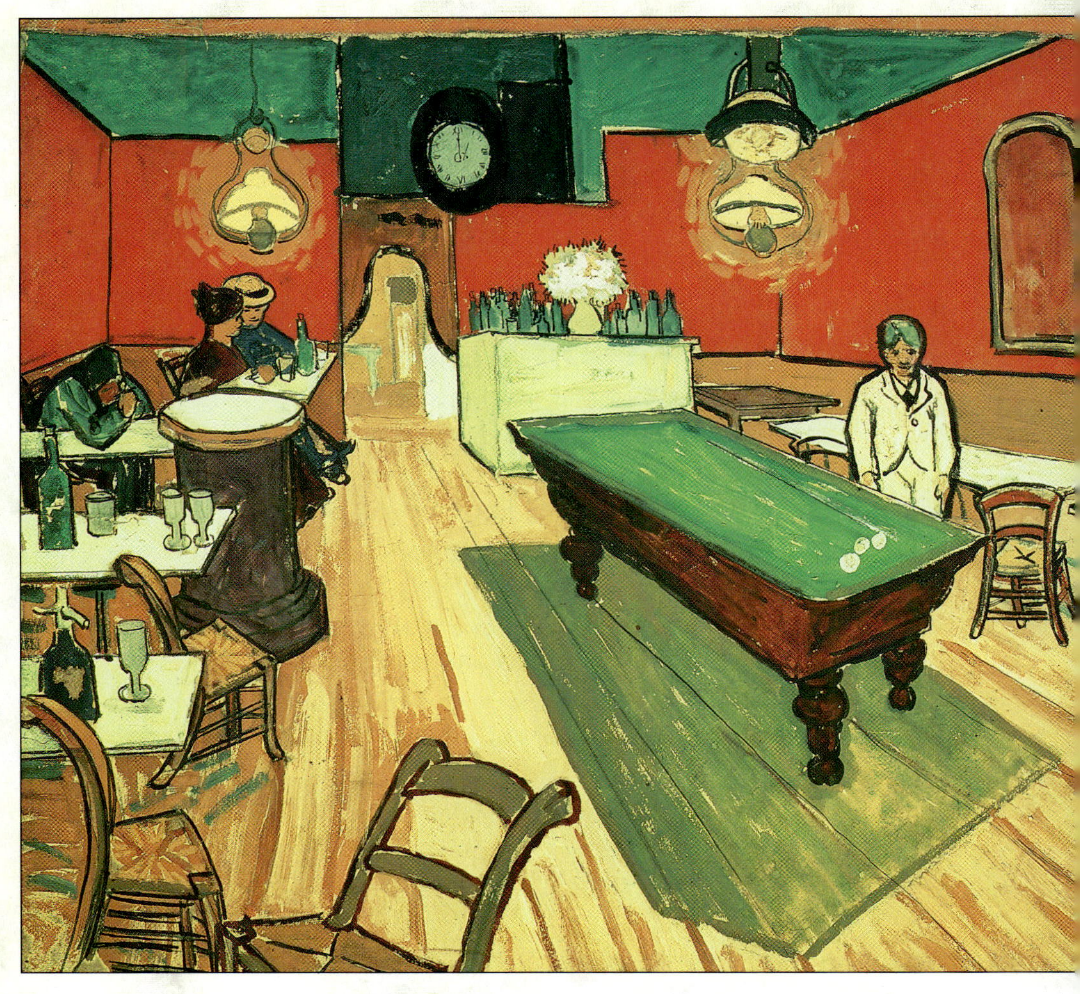

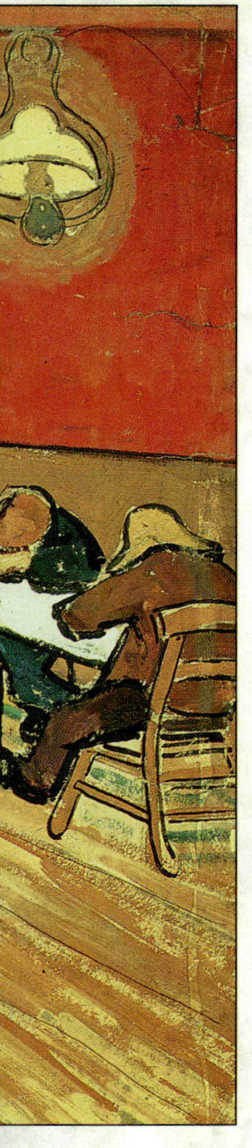

The Night Café

Vincent described *The Night Café* as one of his ugliest pictures. He meant this more in triumph than derision, for he had deliberately set out to create a painting with a crude, nightmarish quality. The work is based on the interior of the Café de l'Alcazar in Arles, where Vincent lodged from May until September 1888. For Vincent and other lost souls such all-night cafés were welcome places of refuge, but also 'a place where one can ruin oneself, go mad or commit a crime'. Vincent hoped to break new ground by expressing the emotional content of the picture through colour alone. He used lurid tones of red, green and 'sulphur' yellow to convey 'an atmosphere like a devil's furnace'. He sent Theo this watercolour copy, eager as usual to keep his brother up to date with his progress.

1888
Watercolour on paper
Private collection

Portrait of Joseph Roulin

Continually seeking new models for his 'modern' portraits, Vincent made friends with the local postman in Arles, Joseph Roulin, who agreed to pose for him on several occasions. Although the kindly Roulin refused payment, he eventually cost Vincent more in food and drink! Nevertheless, the postman became a good friend to the artist, providing support and comfort to him during his bouts of illness.

This was the first of six portraits of Roulin that he completed in a period of nine months. The painting took Vincent just a few days – the speed of execution helping him to create this simple, direct image. Vincent went on to paint Roulin's entire family. He wanted his paintings to express a 'sincere human feeling', and in this he found these ordinary folk ideal subjects.

1888
81 x 65 cm
Oil on canvas
The Museum of Fine Art, Boston

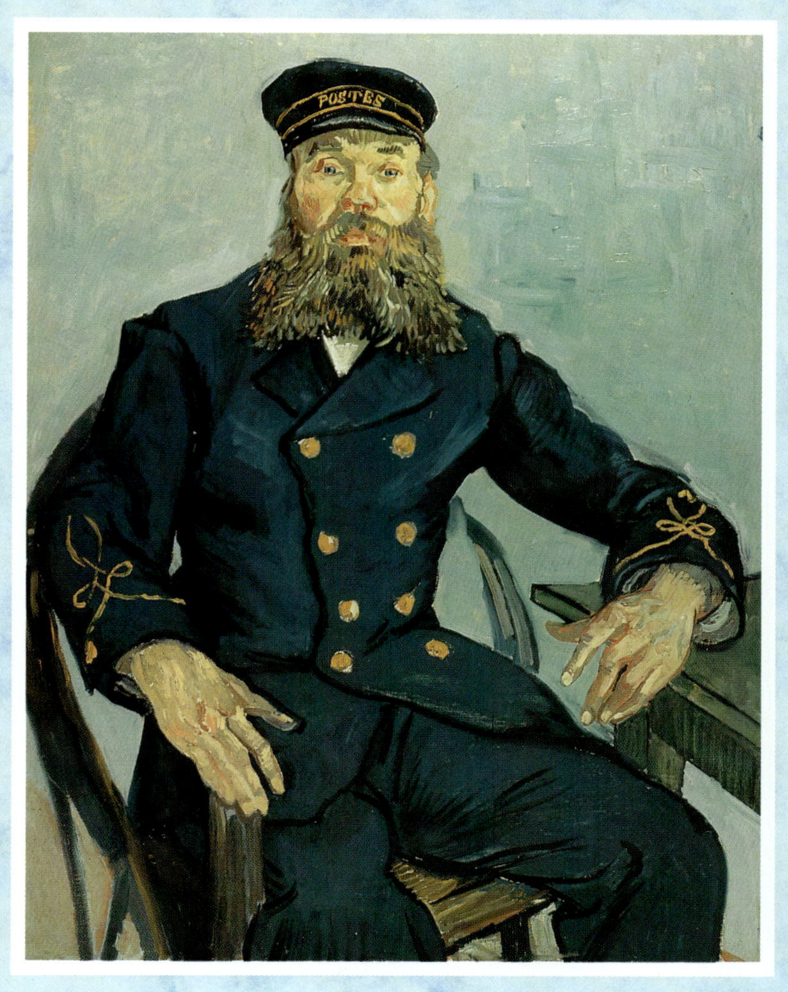
POSTES

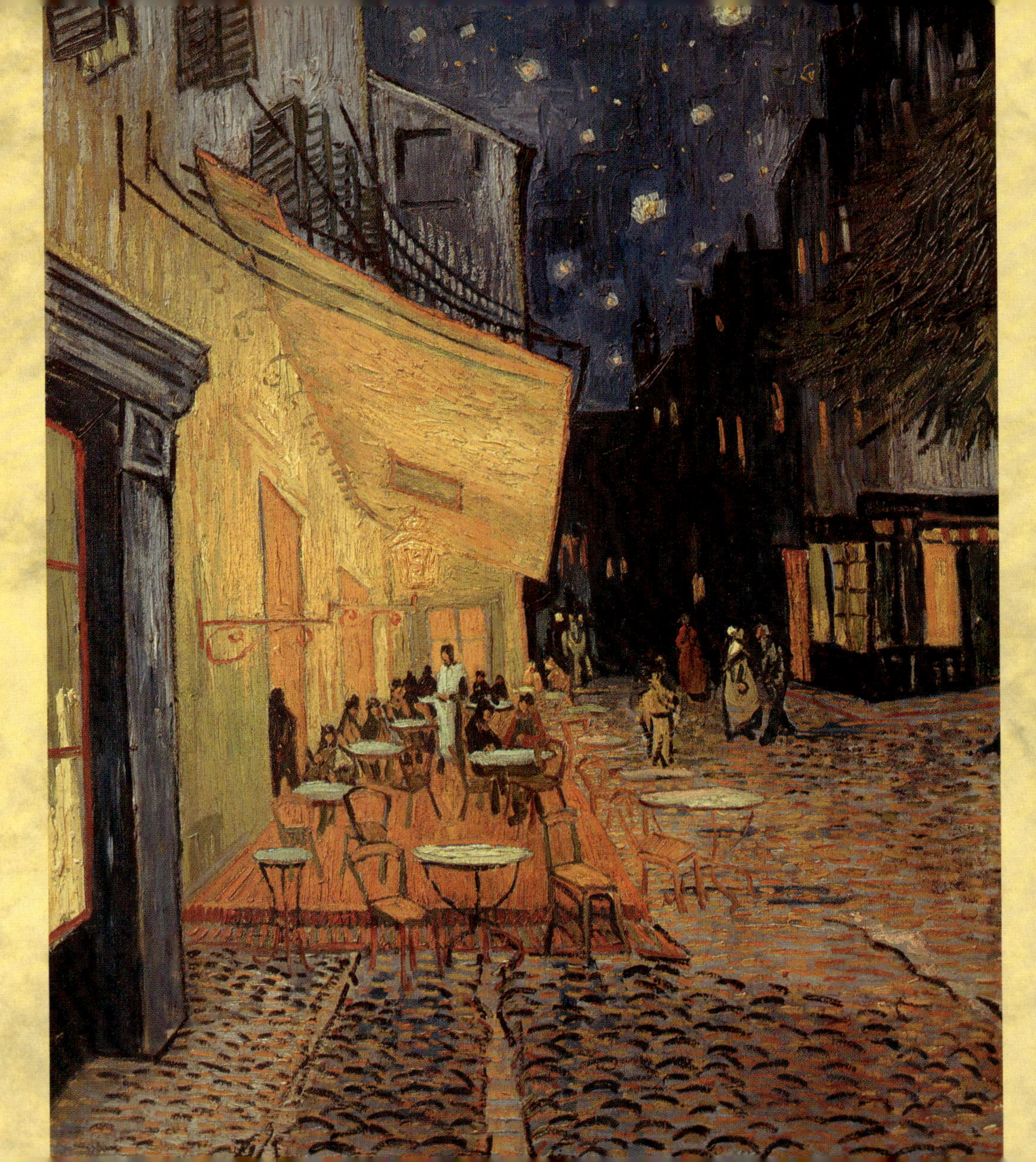

Café Terrace at Night

The idea of painting a night scene had interested Vincent for some time, but he had been undecided as to the exact subject. One evening, as he passed the Grand Café in the centre of Arles, he noticed a dramatic contrast in colour between the warm, yellow rays emanating from the café terrace and the cool, blue light of the starry sky. His problem was solved.

Determined to work on the spot, Vincent set up his easel outside the cafe and ingeniously attached several candles to the brim of his hat so that he could see. The citizens of Arles, having never witnessed such odd behaviour, wondered if they had a madman on their hands! Vincent painted comparatively few views of Arles itself, and was even less inclined to do so once he became known as the town eccentric.

1888
81 x 66 cm
Oil on canvas
Kroller-Muller Museum, Otterlo

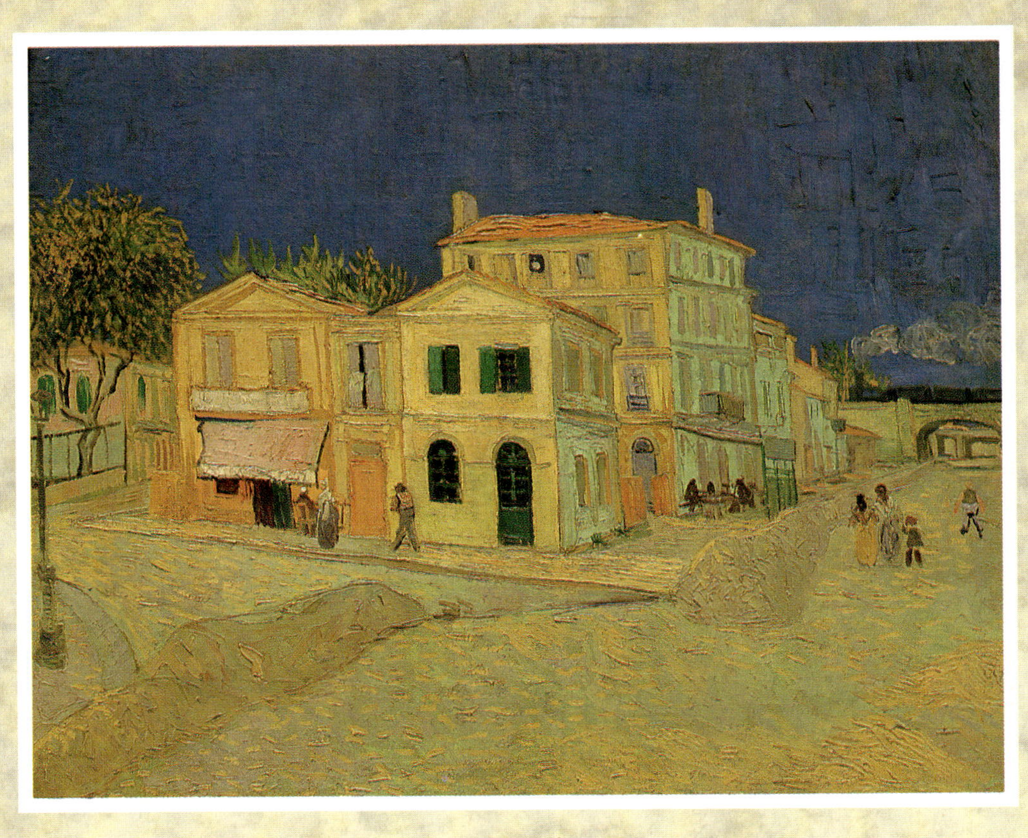

The Yellow House

Renting the Yellow House in the Place Lamartine in Arles was the nearest Vincent came to having a home of his own, and he was immensely proud of it. He painted this sunny picture at the end of September, shortly after moving in.

This tiny building, with its crumbling yellow façade and green shutters, cost Vincent fifteen francs a month – considerably less than his lodgings. He hoped the saving would enable him to set up an artists' colony but, as he discovered, it was not even enough to buy furniture. This delayed his occupancy from May until September, when Theo kindly sent him 300 francs. Vincent did his best to improve the house in readiness for Gauguin's arrival, having decided that his friend would be the first to have the honour of sharing his new home.

1888
72 x 91 cm
Oil on canvas
Vincent van Gogh Museum, Amsterdam

Sunflowers

In August 1888, Vincent began his sunflower series as part of a decorative scheme for Gauguin's bedroom. When hung on the walls, he hoped they would achieve the effect of 'stained-glass windows in a Gothic church'. As the cut flowers died quickly, Vincent rose early to paint them in a single sitting. He just used searing yellows, a colour he associated with love and the great heat of the Provençal sun. The huge blooms, some fresh, others twisted and dying, seem to reflect both sides of Vincent's nature: sunny and dark.

Vincent considered two of the four finished canvases among his finest (this being one), showing them at a Brussels exhibition where they were fairly well received. Even Gauguin, rarely complimentary about Vincent's work, was sufficiently moved to ask for a copy of them.

1888
93 x 73 cm
Oil on canvas
The National Gallery, London

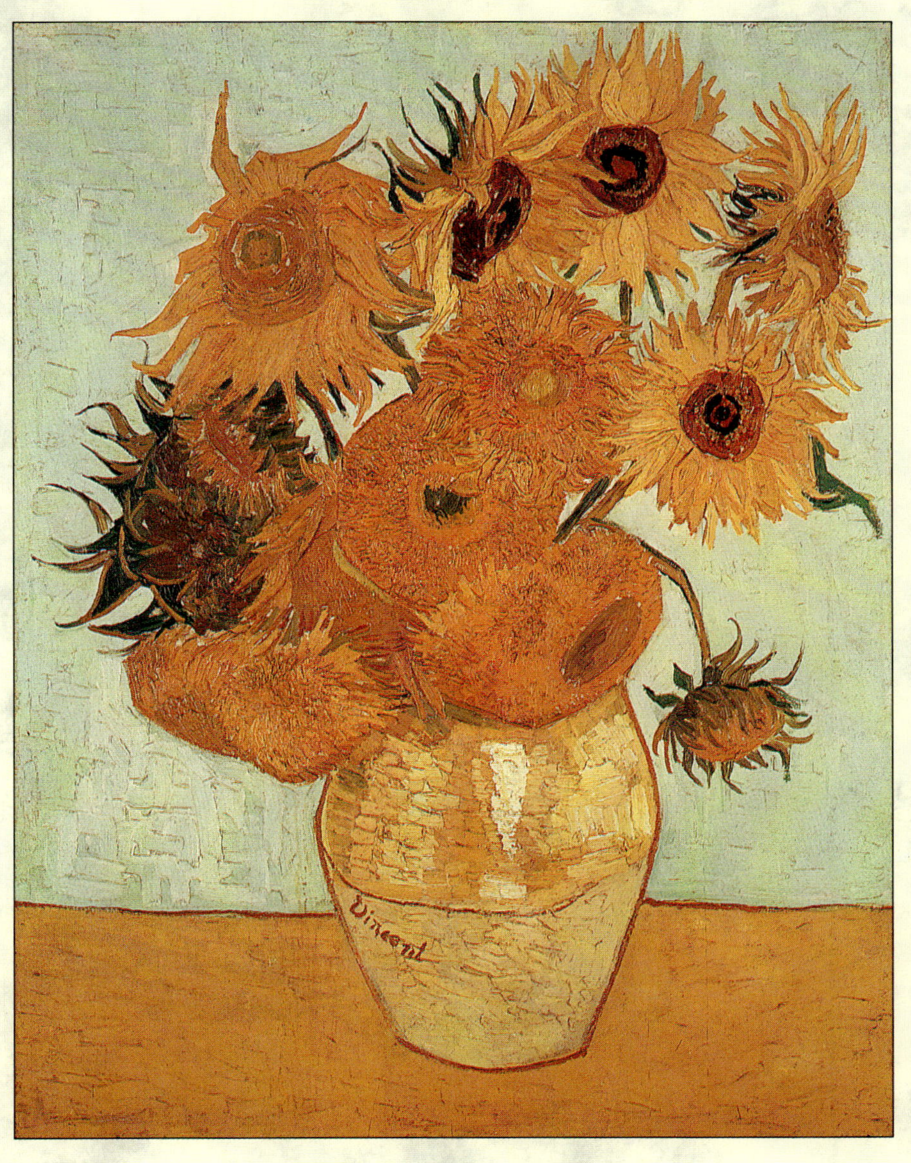
Vincent

The Red Vineyard

On 23 October, 1888, Gauguin joined Vincent in Arles with the added incentive of 150 francs a month from Theo in return for one painting. Vincent was delighted to have the company of the older and more experienced Gauguin – his 'studio of the South' was at last a reality.

The two artists worked side by side, often on the same theme. In November they both completed paintings of vineyards after seeing the effect of a rainstorm at sunset, which made the vines glow 'red like red wine'. Vincent painted his picture to accompany an earlier canvas, *The Green Vineyard*, as part of a series on autumn. It is now largely renowned for being the only painting Vincent sold in his lifetime, bought for 400 Belgian francs by Anna Boch, the sister of Vincent's artist friend Eugene.

1888
73 x 92 cm
Oil on canvas
Pushkin Museum, Moscow

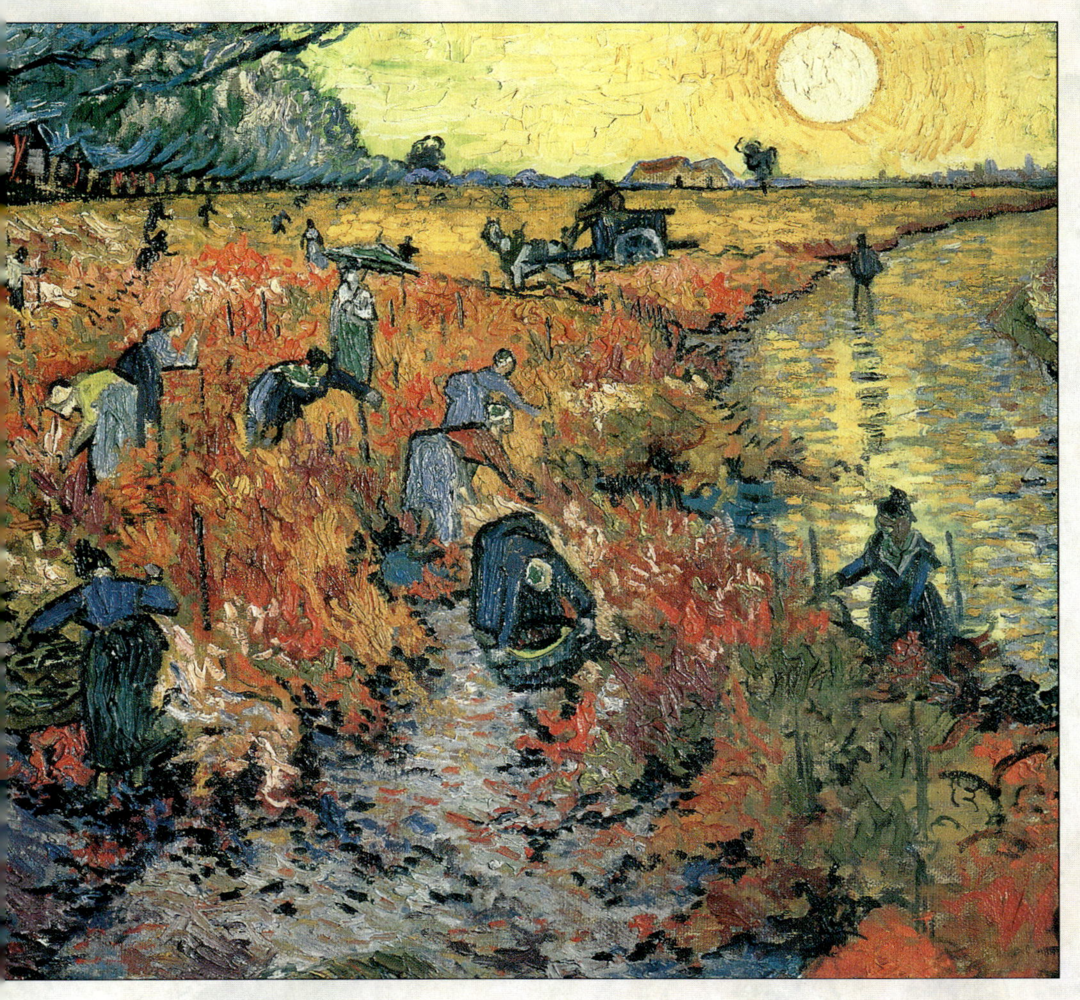

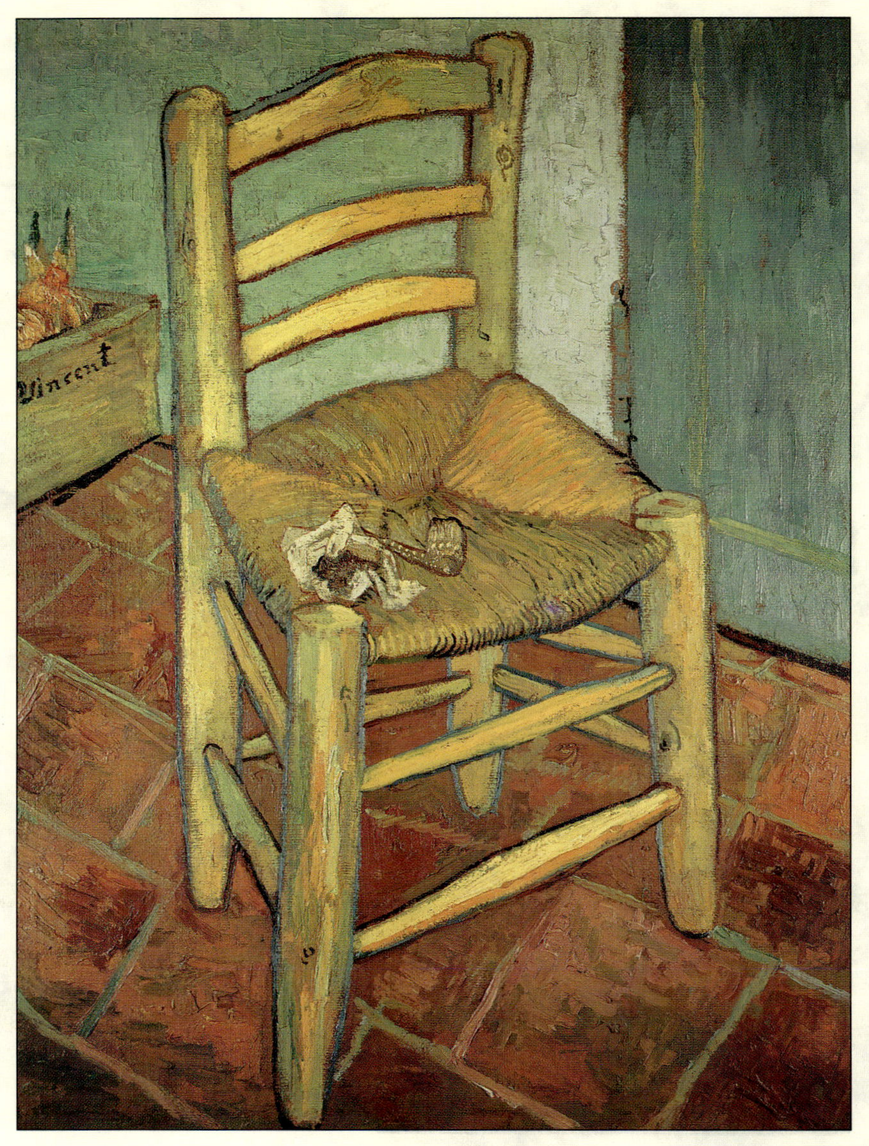
Vincent

Vincent's Chair

This painting and its counterpart, *Gauguin's Chair*, were inspired by an engraving of Charles Dickens' study after his death – his empty chair pushed to one side. Vincent liked the idea of depicting someone's personality through an object, and thought it would be amusing to contrast his and Gauguin's characters in two paintings.

Vincent – a realist in that he painted directly from nature – depicted his simple chair in daylight, against a plain tiled floor and with nothing but his pipe, tobacco and a box of onions. Gauguin's chair, however, he made more elaborate, as befitted a man he held to be a true artist. Since Gauguin worked mostly from his imagination, Vincent showed his chair in artificial light, accompanied by two books and a candle, perhaps to signify his friend's visionary nature.

1888
92 x 73 cm
Oil on canvas
The National Gallery, London

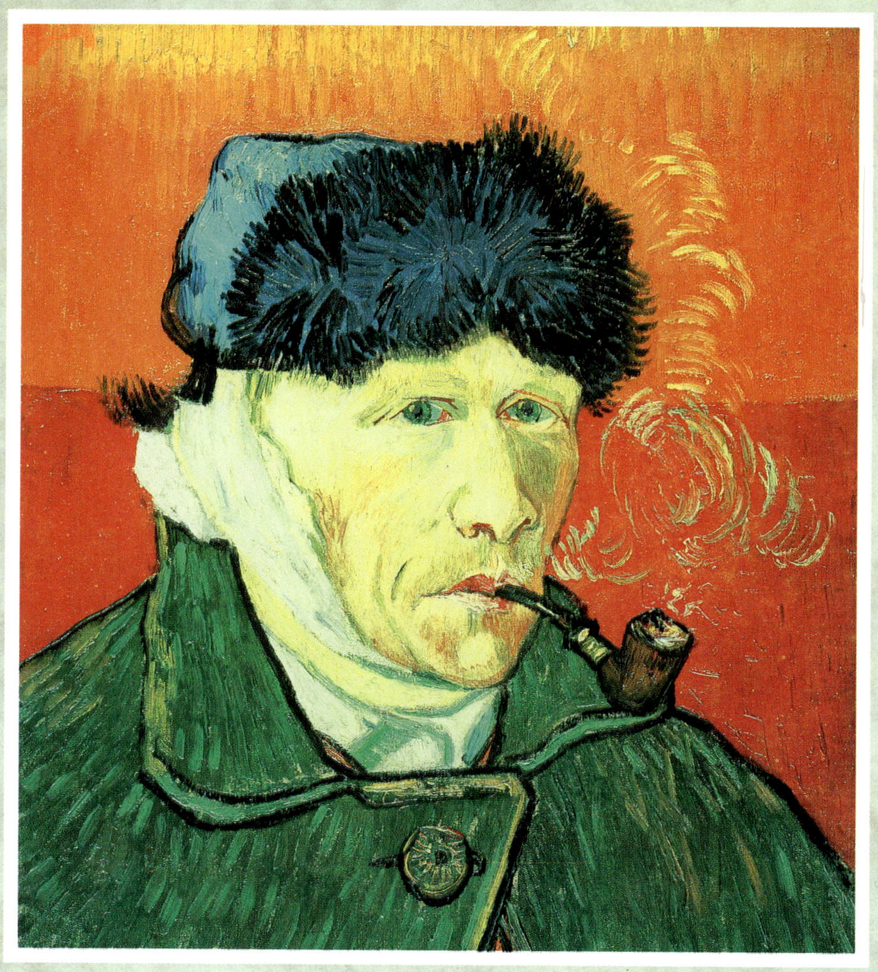

Self-Portrait

Vincent painted this impressive self-portrait after a violent seizure in which he cut off part of his ear. Shortage of models often necessitated the study of his own face, but traumatic events also led to this process of self-examination. On 23 December, following a quarrel with Gauguin, Vincent threatened his friend with a razor, then ran off and severed his own ear, presenting it to a terrified local prostitute with the words, 'Guard this object carefully'! Vincent had feared that Gauguin would leave, and that Theo – now engaged – would also abandon him. This portrait was painted just after leaving hospital and, with its steady gaze, makes a surprisingly bold statement. It was, perhaps, Vincent's way of reasserting his faith in himself, his bandaged ear being the only clue to his terrible ordeal.

1889
51 x 45 cm
Oil on canvas
Private collection

Portrait of Madame Roulin

Before his attack in December, Vincent had been working on a portrait of the postman's wife, Augustine Roulin, rocking her baby's cradle. After the torment of his mental breakdown this tender image of motherly love, with its suggestion of comfort and security, had special significance for Vincent, and he made no less than four copies of the original, this being one.

In Vincent's mind the painting acquired almost religious status. He thought of displaying it like an altarpiece with the portrait forming the centre panel, flanked by two of his sunflower still lifes which he said expressed 'gratitude'. Vincent was certainly grateful to Madame Roulin, not only for being his model, but also for the kindness she showed him during his illness. In simple thanks, he gave her a copy of the portrait.

1889
92 x 72cm
Oil on canvas
The Chicago Art Institute

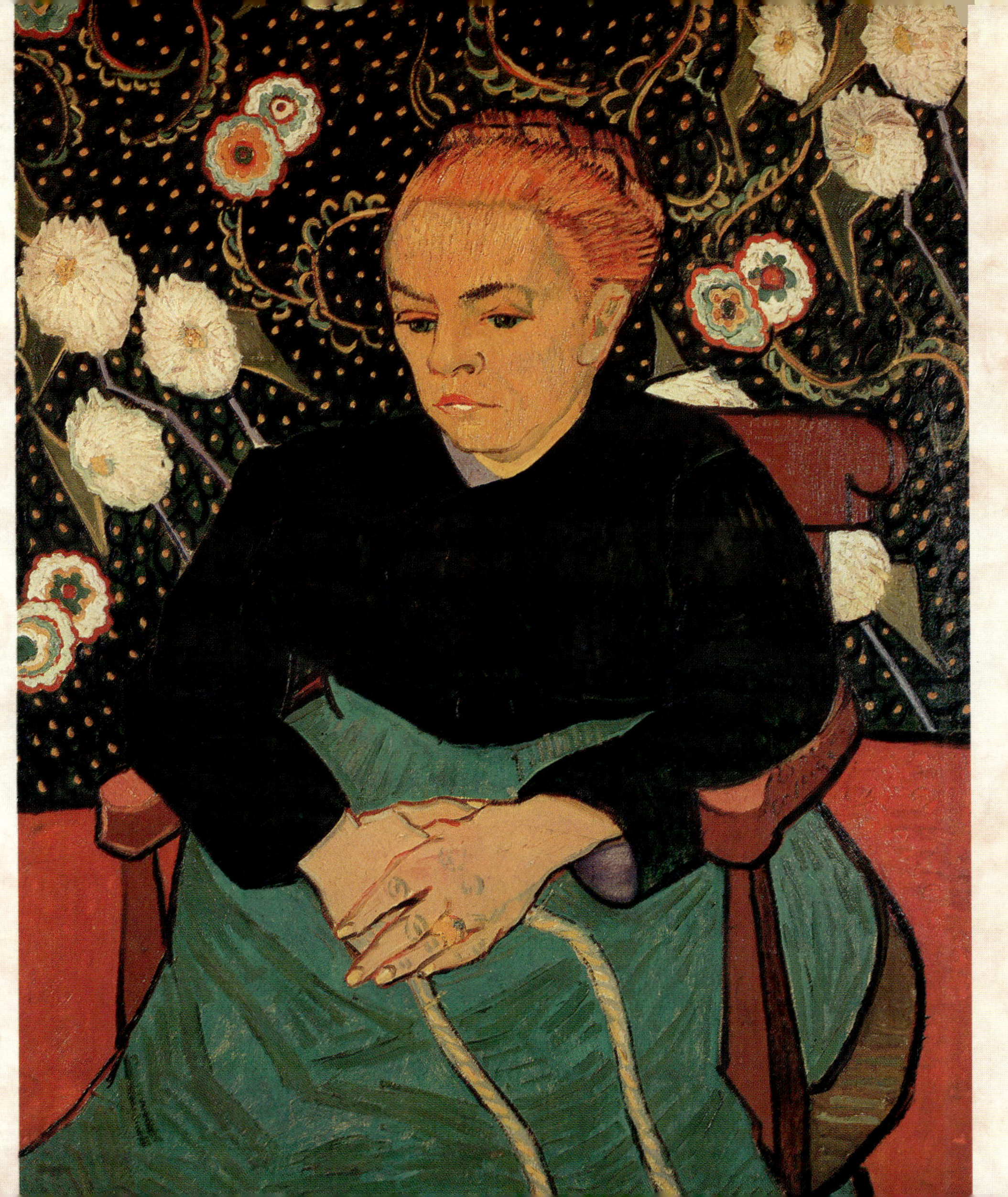

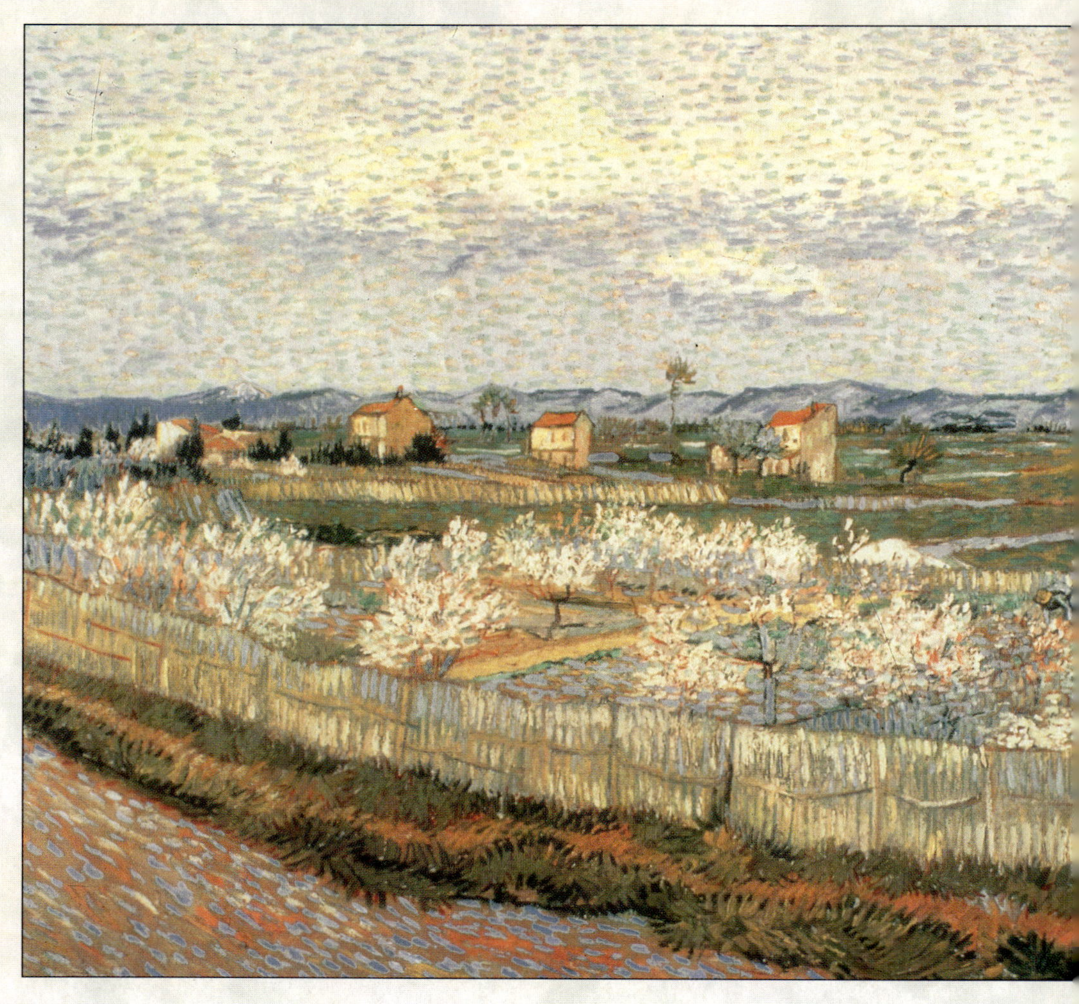

Peach Trees in the Crau

In February and March 1889, Vincent suffered further bouts of mental illness. At times he was almost delirious, convinced he was being poisoned. For his own safety, he was taken back to hospital. Once his condition improved Vincent eagerly resumed his work, returning to the blossom-filled valley of the Crau. He painted this delicate landscape at the end of March, shortly after a visit from his old friend, Paul Signac. The tiny scale of the houses and fields against the vast southern sky reminded Vincent of 'certain Japanese landscapes', and this was the main reason for his interest in the view. The small flecks of paint are reminiscent of Signac's style, suggesting that his friend was not far from Vincent's thoughts when he worked on this.

1889
66 x 82 cm
Oil on canvas
The Courtauld Institute, London

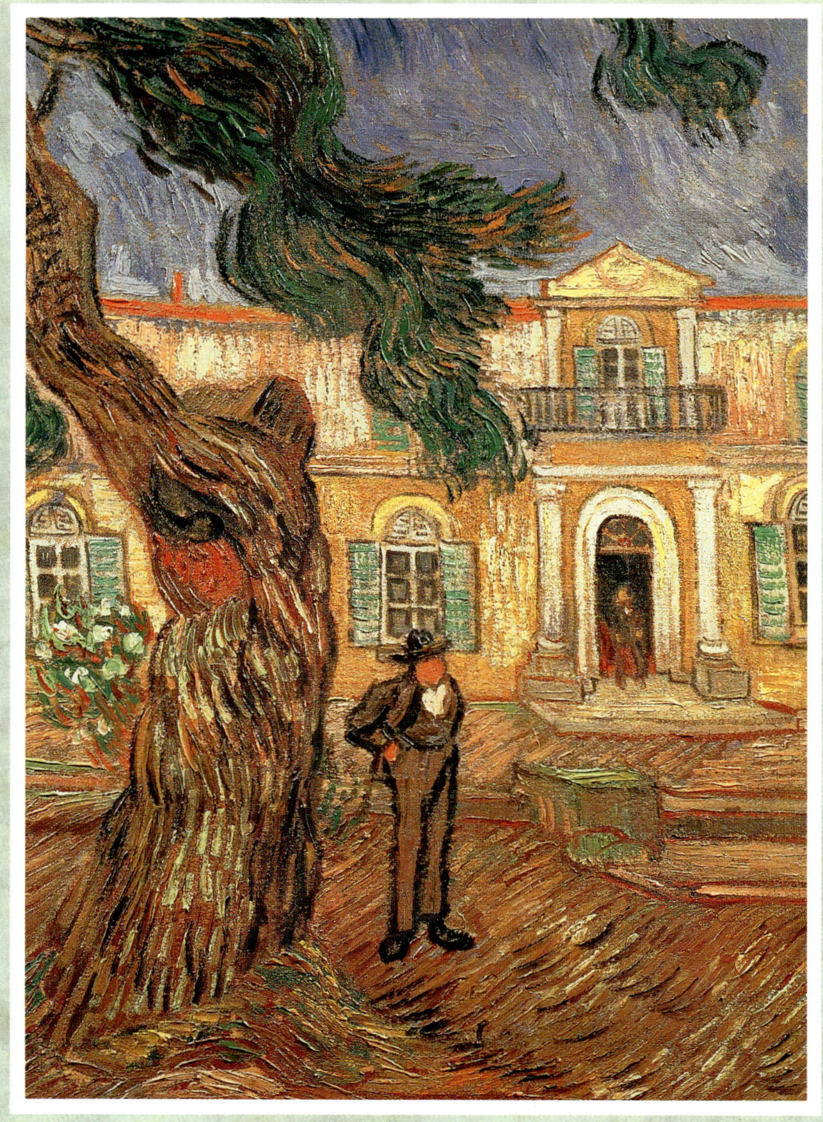

Saint-Rémy Asylum

On 8 May, 1889, Vincent was admitted as a voluntary patient to Saint-Rémy asylum, a few miles northeast of Arles. He had been forced to close down the Yellow House after thirty of his neighbours, fearing they had a madman in their midst, signed a petition demanding his removal. The privately run asylum provided a safe haven, somewhere he could work in peace and receive specialist care. This was often needed, as when he attempted suicide by swallowing his paints!

Vincent made several paintings from different angles of the somewhat dilapidated exterior of his new home. Under the gigantic, twisting pine tree stands Dr Peyron, the director of the asylum, who treated Vincent, diagnosing his illness as epilepsy rather than madness. The small figure in the doorway is probably Vincent himself.

1889
58 x 45 cm
Oil on canvas
Musée d'Orsay, Paris

Irises

At Saint-Rémy asylum Vincent was given his own bedroom, a scantily furnished cell with barred windows, and a spare room to use as a studio. The latter overlooked the garden, where he painted this rich and beautiful study of irises. This was the first of his paintings at Saint-Rémy and shows that his attacks of insanity left his artistic ability unimpaired. Its simplicity belies its skilled composition – it would be less effective without the single white iris, for instance. Many of Vincent's flower paintings were intended as technical exercises, but the more finished pieces, such as this, he signed, knowing that there was usually a ready market for floral subjects. Although the canvas was exhibited at the 1889 Salon des Indépendants, where the critic Fénéon admired it, *Irises* failed to sell.

1889
73 x 94 cm
Oil on canvas
Private collection

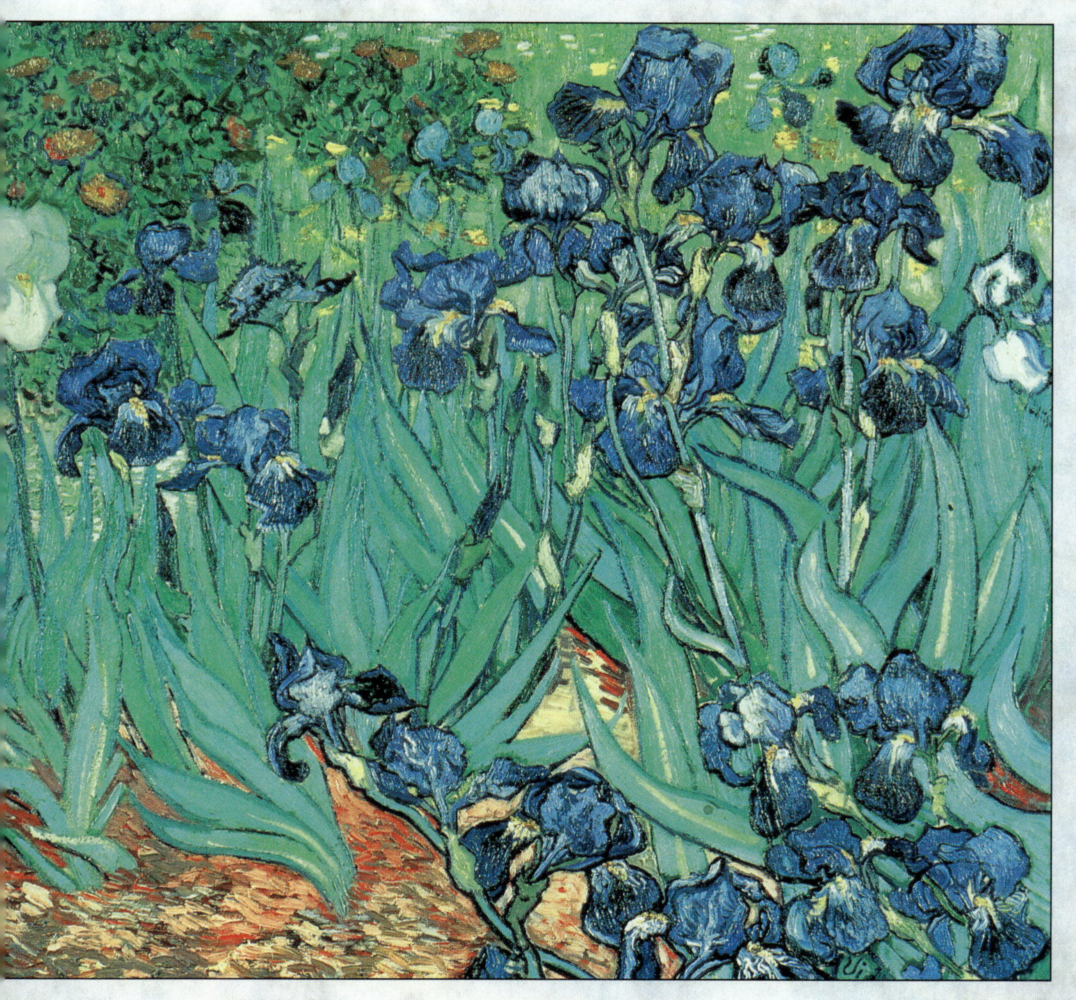

Wheatfield with Cypresses

Everything is on the move in this moody landscape of a windswept summer's day. Vincent used loose brushstrokes to describe the billowing clouds and swirling vegetation – even the Alpilles Mountains in the middle distance seem to ebb and flow like a choppy sea. The small bush to the centre provides the eye's only resting point.

As Vincent's health improved he was allowed to work further afield. Accompanied by an attendant in case of a fit, he explored the countryside around Saint-Rémy. He was fascinated by the dramatic shape of the cypresses silhouetted against the blue sky. Like his *Sunflowers*, they became an important, if slightly sinister, symbol of Provence for him. Vincent was so pleased with the work that he produced a smaller version for his mother and sister.

1889
72 x 91 cm
Oil on canvas
The National Gallery, London

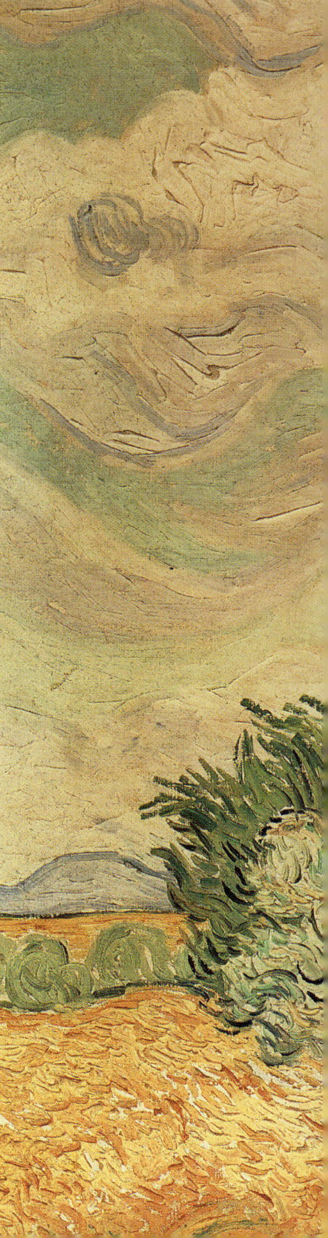

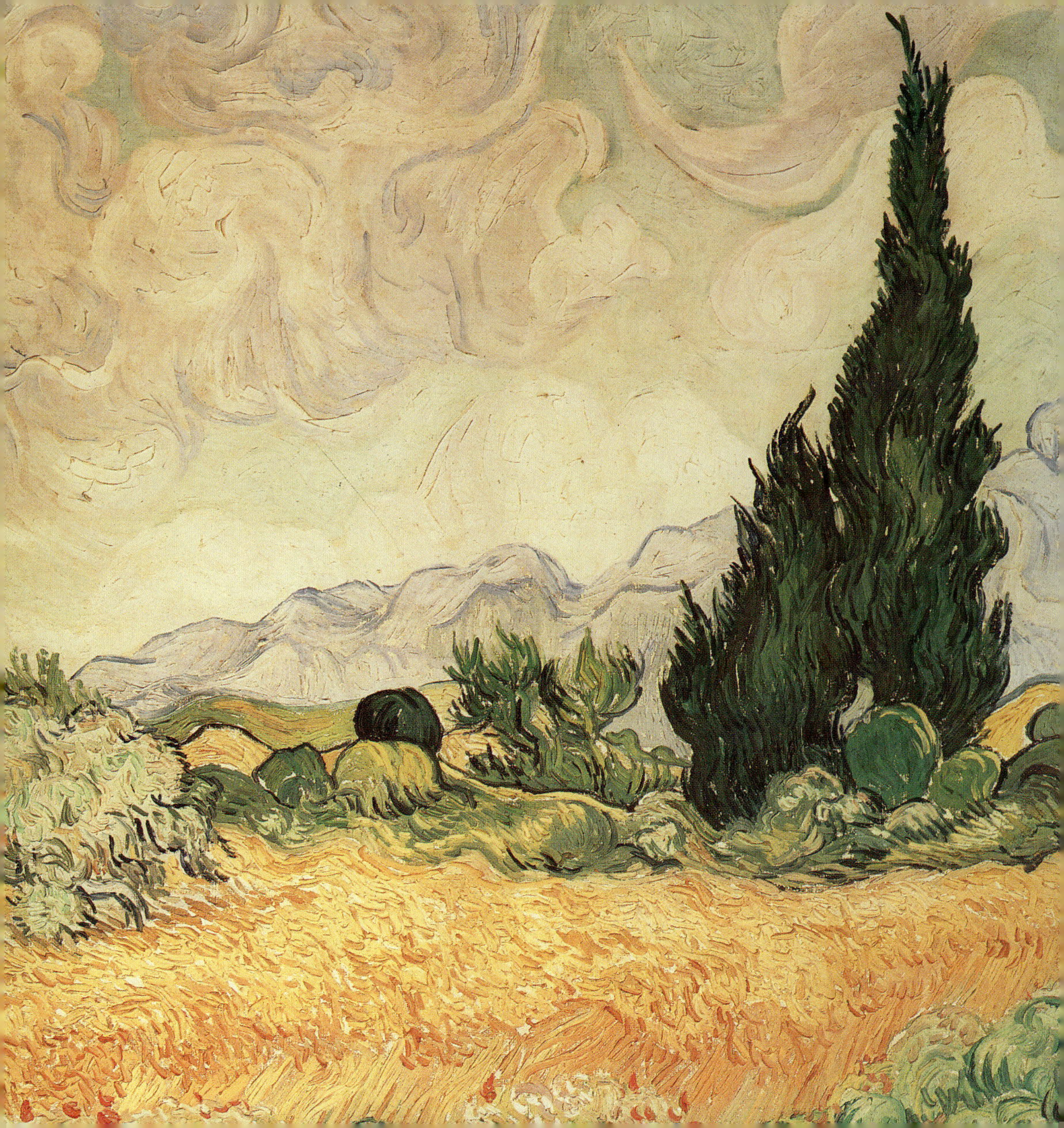

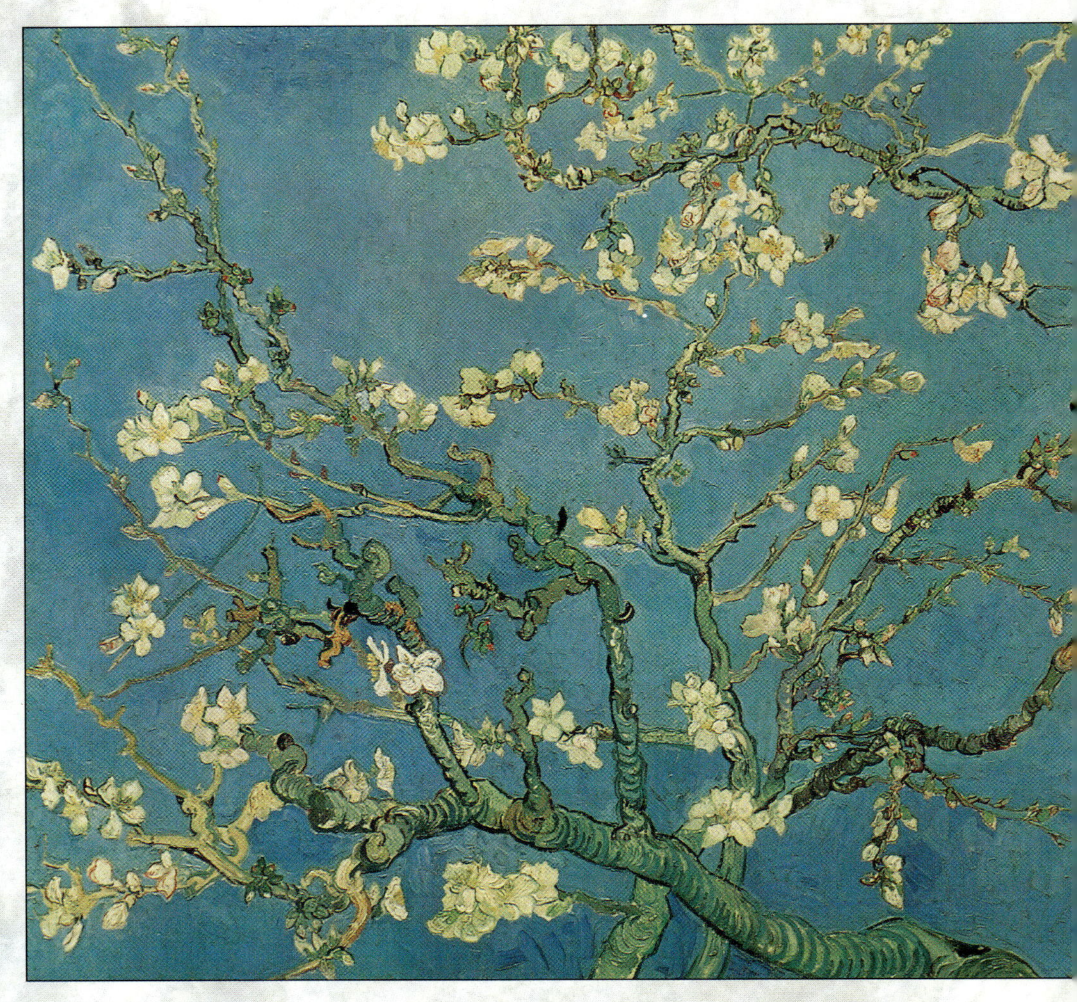

Branches with Almond Blossom

Vincent painted these almond branches bursting with new life to celebrate the birth of his nephew on 31 January, 1890. The early flowering almond tree was one of Vincent's favourite subjects and made an appropiate gift for the young boy who had been named after him. He cleverly painted the white blossoms from below, as a child lying in a cradle might see them.

Whilst Vincent was pleased for Theo and his wife, the birth was a reminder of his own situation. He realised he was unlikely to know such happiness himself. The day after he completed the painting, he had another breakdown lasting several months. By May he felt better, but the blossoms were over and he could not continue the series as he had intended. To be nearer to Theo, he moved to Auvers, just outside Paris.

1890
74 x 92 cm
Oil on canvas
Vincent van Gogh Museum, Amsterdam

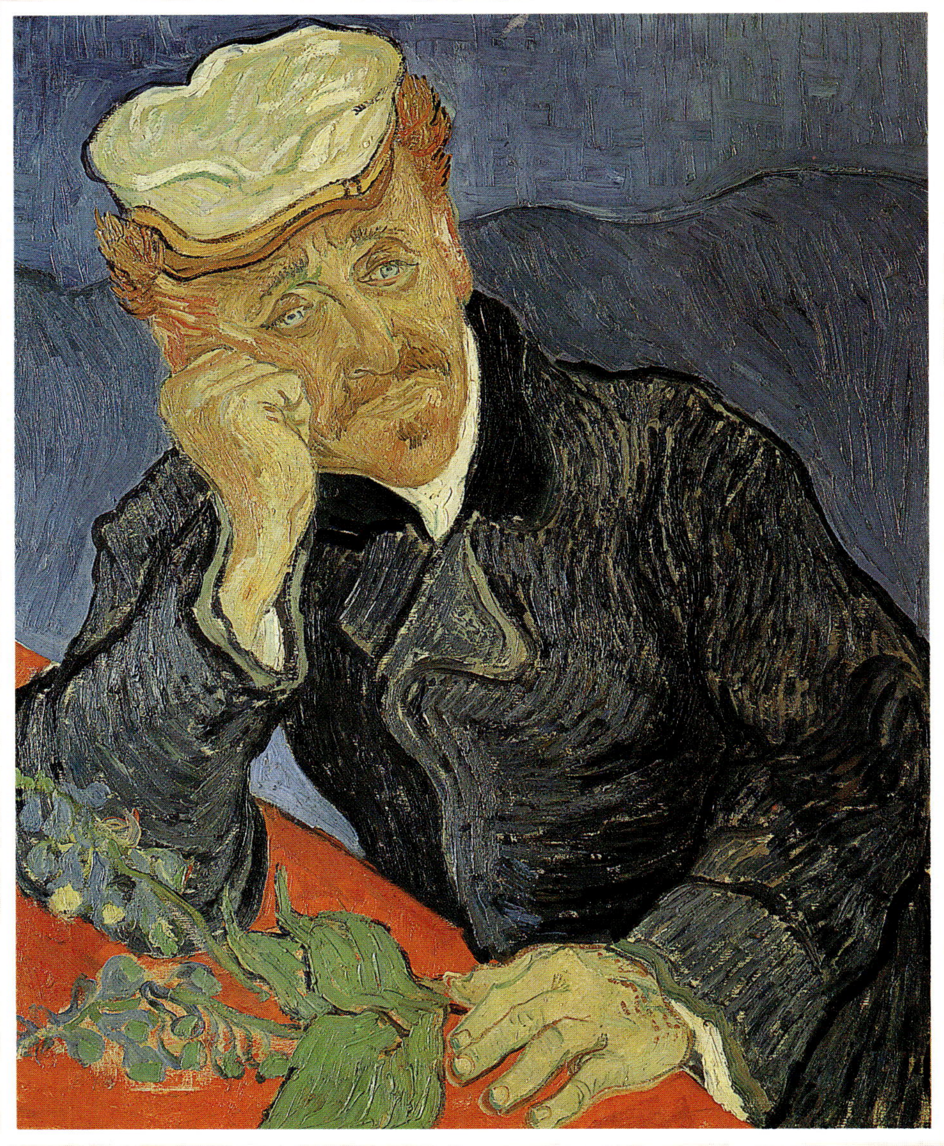

Dr Paul Gachet

In Auvers Vincent was put in the care of Dr Gachet, a homeopathic physician and art lover, who specialised in nervous disorders and became a good friend to the artist. This is the second of two portraits completed at Gachet's request. The painting could almost be a self-portrait, so much did the two men resemble each other in appearance and temperament. Certainly, Gachet's kind forgiving expression of gentle melancholy gives some clue as to why Vincent found him such sympathetic company. In fact, achieving an exact likeness was less important to Vincent than the overall feeling of the painting. By giving the portrait passion and expression he hoped to make it 'live' – not just for him at the time, but for future generations.

1890
68 x 57 cm
Oil on canvas
Musee d'Orsay, Paris

Cottages at Auvers

Shortly after arriving in Auvers, Vincent settled into his familiar pattern of rising early and working until dusk, in this way averaging a painting a day. The thatched cottages lining the village streets soon caught his attention, and he told Theo he hoped to paint them. This canvas may have been inspired by a similar painting by the French artist, Daubigny, who had lived and worked in Auvers. Indeed, Vincent's admiration for the painter was one reason why the village so attracted him.

Vincent used a new, elongated format in his Auvers landscapes, consisting of a double square, which gave him more scope for panoramic views. His approach was as spontaneous as ever, as can be seen by the short, sharp brushstrokes in this unfinished, but still appealing, canvas.

1890
50 x 100 cm
Oil on canvas
The Tate Gallery, London

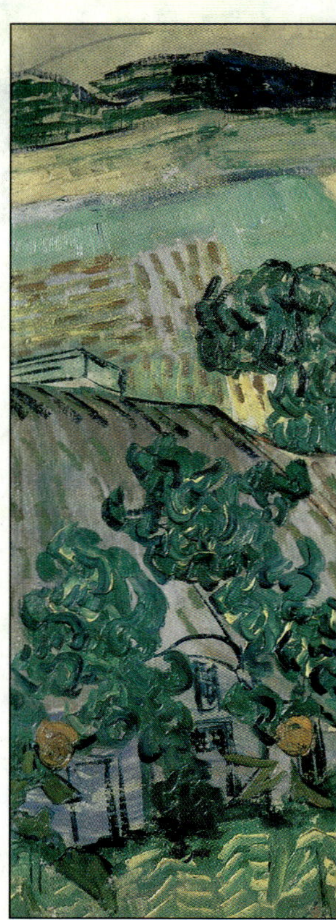

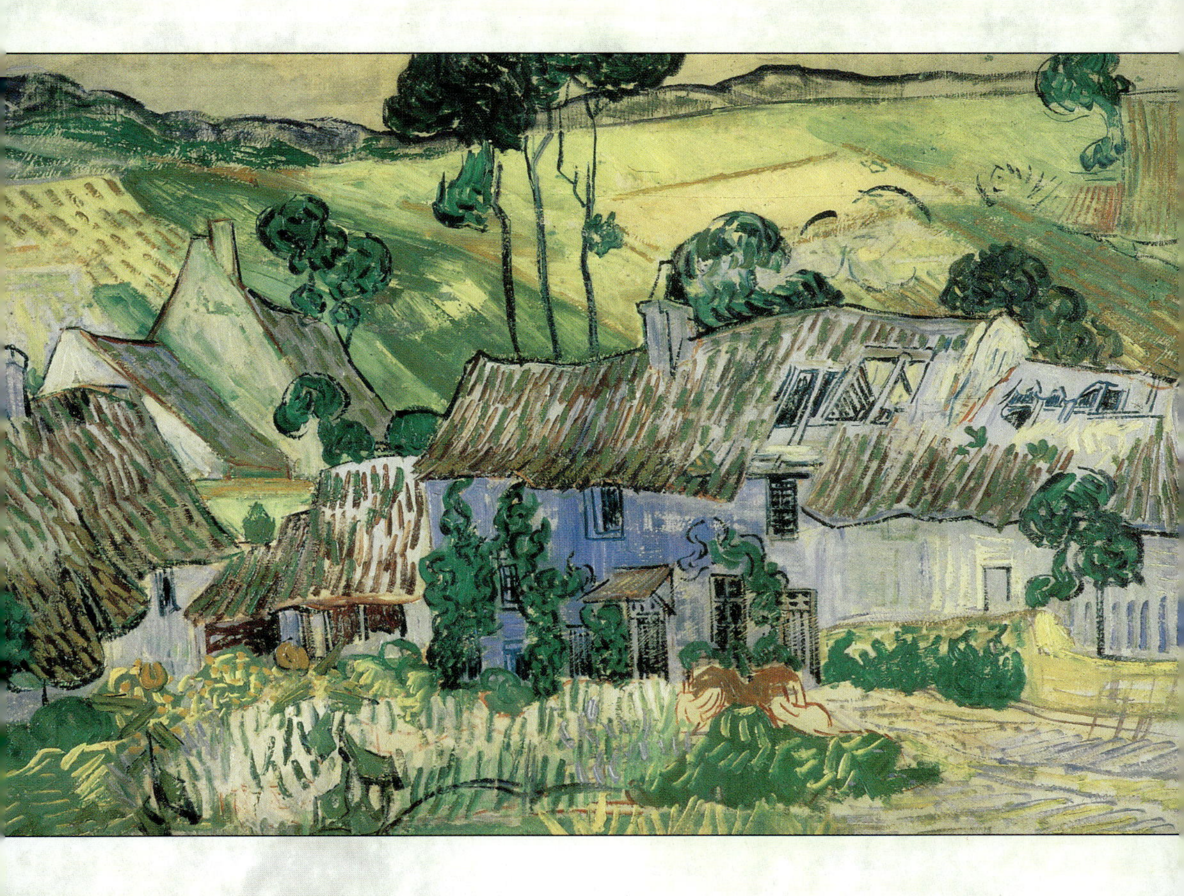

The Church at Auvers

The summer Vincent painted the little Gothic church in Auvers, his thoughts were turning towards home. The church reminded him of the old tower near his parents' house at Nuenen, which he had painted five years earlier, and even the woman to the left is Dutch in appearance.

The heavy blue sky gives the painting a brooding, melancholy character, matched by Vincent's mood at this time. Feeling lonely and depressed, and a burden to Theo, he had even begun to doubt his artistic abilities. Though he had sacrificed everything for his painting, he had received little critical recognition. In total despair, he shot himself on 27 July, dying two days later in Theo's arms.

The priests of Auvers church refused to hold his funeral service as he had taken his own life.

1890
94 x 74 cm
Oil on canvas
Musée d'Orsay, Paris

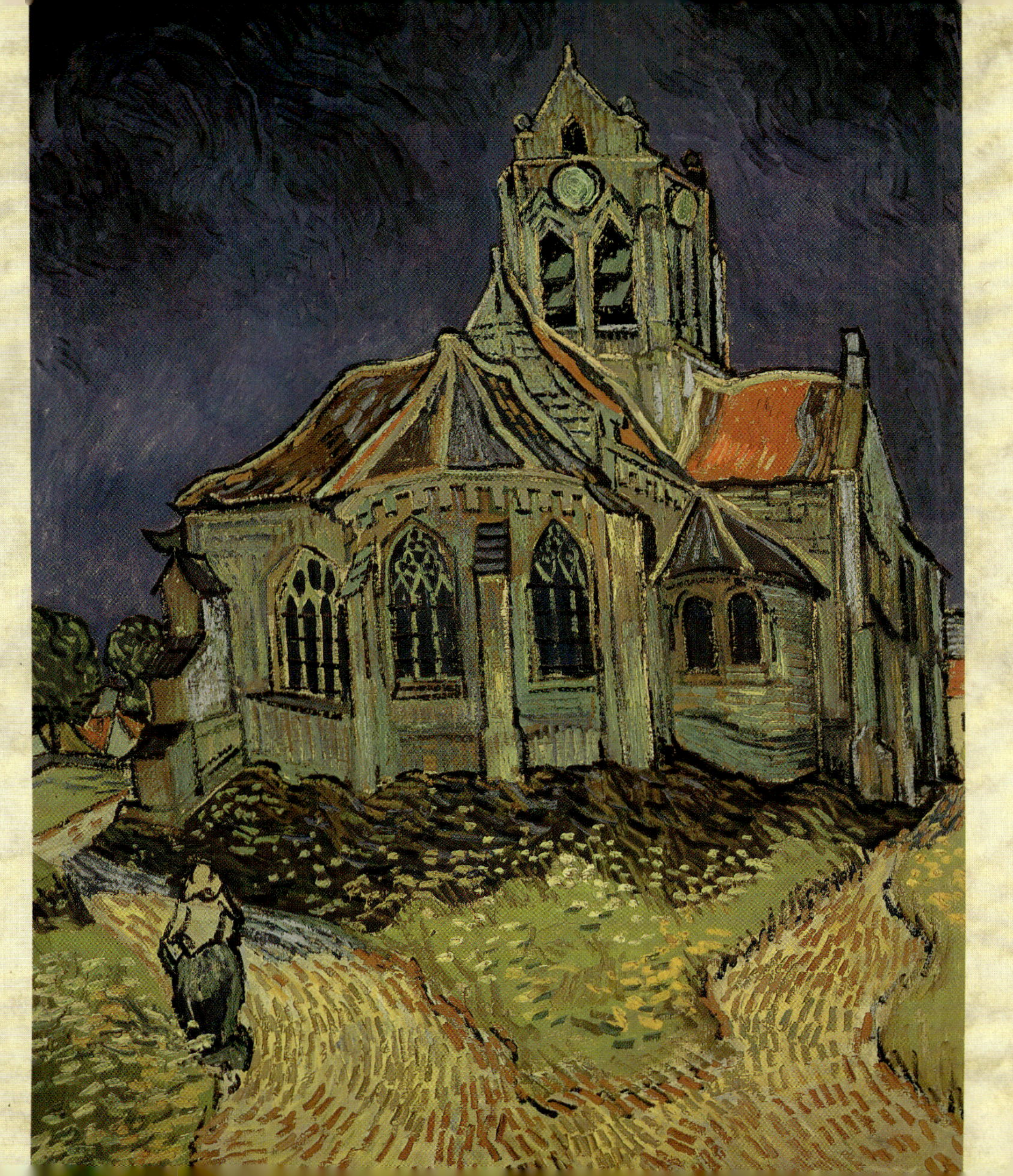

Acknowledgements

The publishers would like to thank the following for permission to reproduce:–

A.K.G., Berlin, for the jacket and pp. 14, 18, 20-21, 26-27, 35, 40, 43, 48-49;

Art Resource, New York, for the back flap and pp. 22-23, 24, 30, 38, 52-53, 54, 59;

The Bridgeman Art Library, London, for pp. 12-13, 16-17, 29, 36-37, 44-45, 46, 50-51, 56-57;

Picturepoint, Windsor, for the title page, last page and pp. 10, 32.

Title page and facing page: *Self Portrait*
Chicago Art Institute
Back flap: *Gauguin's Chair*
Vincent van Gogh Museum, Amsterdam